Global Responsibility

Hans Küng

Global Responsibility

*In Search of a New
World Ethic*

CROSSROAD • NEW YORK

1991

The Crossroad Publishing Company
370 Lexington Avenue, New York, NY 10017

Translated from the German *Projekt Weltethos*
Published by R. Piper GmbH & Co. KG, Munich 1990
Copyright © Hans Küng 1990
English translation copyright © John Bowden 1991

Printed in the United States of America

Library of Congress Catalog Card Number: 91–7956
ISBN: 0-8245-1102-6

For Karl and Ilse Klasen

Contents

Preface by His Royal Highness the Duke of Edinburgh, KG

Anyone who takes even a cursory interest in the state of our planet's health and vitality must be aware that things are going badly wrong. They are going wrong, not because there are some evil and destructive forces at work, but simply because people are behaving naturally. The world's human population has been growing at an ever-increasing rate, and the more people there are on this limited globe, the more space we occupy, the more resources we consume, the more waste and pollution we produce and the more damage we do to the planet's natural systems when we indulge in civil, political and religious conflict.

Some people may respond to rational scientific arguments, but I am convinced that it needs more than that. It is one thing to understand the problems, it is quite another to have the will to implement practical remedies, particularly if they demand restraint and sacrifice. The motivation for altruism seems to originate in a personal attachment to an ideology or to a religion. The evidence suggests that people are influenced in their behaviour by moral conviction and ethical concepts. People are more likely to go to the stake for their beliefs than for their knowledge of the facts. While it has proved possible to arrive at a broad consensus about the facts of life on earth, so far at least, it has proved impossible to overcome the jealousies, rivalries and the destructive consequences of competing religions and ideologies.

Hans Küng points out in his introduction, ' . . . the one world in which we live has a chance of survival only if there is no longer any room in it for spheres of differing, contradictory and even antagonistic ethics'. In this book, he has chosen to discuss what is probably the most critical and challenging issue in the debate about the future of the human habitation of this globe. I very much hope that this scholarly contribution will help to stimulate a more determined search for a shared belief in the beauty and value of this planet Earth as our common and unique home in the vastness of the universe.

Introduction

No survival without a world ethic. No world peace without peace between the religions. No peace between the religions without dialogue between the religions. That is what this book is about.

It is certainly a short book, but there is a long history behind it. I would not have dared to write on the theme of a world ethic had I not previously worked on the theoretical hermeneutical basis for such an ethic and also on its content.[1] By this I mean far more than the world religions with which this book is primarily (but by no means exclusively) concerned and on which I have been able to present studies of my own, in collaboration with qualified colleagues.[2] This basis also includes the evaluation of religion generally: it means coming to terms with modern criticism of religion, secular ethics and the political, social and cultural situation.[3]

So what I have written here on ethics and religion, set out as clearly as possible and written in non-technical language, has been constantly reflected on and tested to the point that it can now be presented with programmatic brevity and sometimes in the form of theses so terse as to be almost scholastic. Here is a provisional attempt to analyse the present revolution of our time and the epoch-making overall constellation which is already coming into view, the new macro-paradigm, which for me is a key concept of universal history. Certainly, given the mass of information (which is said to be doubling every five years) and the daily flood of innovations, the individual may be becoming increasingly 'stupid', but for that very reason we now need a basic orientation in knowledge in order to be able to sort out the confusing details and take them in. I offer such an orientation here. Of course I am also aware that reality is infinitely more complicated, that there are also exceptions to, deviations from, and counter-movements against, all developments and that every detailed statement can be questioned again and again. But it is more important for me that in matters of public concern the public also has a right to be addressed by academics and scientists on the spiritual and cultural situation of the time in clear, understandable language, without convoluted technical jargon and overqualifications which claim to be profundity.

This programmatic work would never have been written had there not been demands arising directly out of the present. All the insights that I have been able to collect through study, and also through journeys in all the major cultural and economic areas of our planet and through encounters with people of very different religions, races and classes, are set down here with the utmost brevity: they indicate the need for an ethic for the whole of the human race. It has become increasingly clear to me in recent years that the one world in which we live has a chance of survival only if there is no longer any room in it for spheres of differing, contradictory and even antagonistic ethics. This one world needs one basic ethic. This one world society certainly does not need a unitary religion and a unitary ideology, but it does need some norms, values, ideals and goals to bring it together and to be binding on it.

I am not concerned here with party politics; as a theologian, precisely at the point when I have to take up a position politically, I feel obligated to the whole and not to any party. And as an ecumenical theologian, although I have a home in my own church, I feel responsible towards all churches and religions: the unity of the churches and peace among the religions. Was it not always the business of religions continually to provide new motivation for people all over the globe towards norms, values, ideals and goals? Despite the fact that religions have two faces - a fact which I myself have experienced enough - that cannot be denied. Moreover in this book I shall not advance any idealistic concept of religion; I shall not transfigure the religions. But the time is ripe for an invitation: at the present moment the world religions have a quite special responsibility for world peace. And the credibility of all religions, including the smaller ones, will in future depend on their putting more stress on what unites them and less on what divides them. For humankind can less and less afford religions stirring up wars on this earth instead of making peace; making people fanatical instead of seeking reconciliation; practising superiority instead of engaging in dialogue.

I have been able to test the programme I set out here in public on countless occasions. Two of them were a special challenge for me. In February 1989 there was a UNESCO symposium on the theme 'No World Peace without Religious Peace', for which the German mission at UNESCO and the Goethe Institute had overall responsibility. I was invited to provided the basic report for this enterprise, and that has now also found a way into this book. Representatives of all the great world religions were invited to this symposium; they responded to my basic paper, so that it was possible for a fruitful dialogue to come about. The second occasion - in the midst of the upheavals in Eastern Europe in February 1990 - was the World Economic Forum in Davos. I am grateful to the founder and president of the World Economic Forum, Professor Klaus Schwab, for challenging me to speak to this international representative body as a theologian. But I am convinced that unless we succeed in also winning over representatives of politics, business and the financial world for this ethical programme, all the ethical demands of religion and the churches, however well meant, will fall on deaf ears. The theme of my Davos lecture was: 'Why do we need global ethical standards to survive?' That manuscript, too, has been worked into the present book; subsequently it was tested in a very different context at the universities of Tübingen and Kiel in public discussion with philosophers like Professor Hans Jonas and Professor Karl-Otto Apel.

The third part of this book is directed entirely towards the future. I have headed it 'Prolegomena', 'Provisional Comments', on a new research project which since 1989 has been made possible for me by the Robert Bosch Jubilee Foundation, and which is devoted to the theme 'No World Peace without Peace between the Religions'. Its aim is an overall theological diagnosis of the religious situation of our time. In the next five years I want to make studies of the religious situation primarily of Judaism, Christianity and Islam. In the third part of this book I have described the analytical concept through which I want to approach this extraordinarily complex undertaking. I have been able to see how the theological analysis of paradigms which I have already suggested[4] is an admirable instrument to apply to the three great currents of the religious systems of humankind; it helps us to understand the present conflicts in each of the religions not only in a wider historical context and in periods of epoch-making change but also in the present-day structuring of their content, and to arrive at possibilities for solutions in the future.

Of course I am fully aware of my own limitations in this short book; after all, this is a complex and wide-ranging inter-disciplinary enterprise, and therefore is open to attack from all sides. That is why I have been cautious over the title. The German original was entitled *Projekt Weltethos* and the English title is similarly tentative. For it would be absurd to think that an individual theologian could simply create something like an 'ethic for the world', or even peace between the religions. But it is the task of the ecumenical theologian in particular to bring to general awareness the common understandings that are already present and continually to insist that in future religions should stress what they have in common more strongly than what divides them. And in ethics the world religions are now closer together than they are in 'dogma'.

In 1990 a book of mine was published entitled *Reforming the Church Today*. In its retrospective approach it was more as it were a programmatic work on 'domestic policy' in the various Christian churches. The present book, however, prepared at the same time, is a programmatic work in anticipation of further publications on 'foreign policy' with a view to the different regions and religions of the world. It will have achieved its aim if it succeeds in two things:

• That an increasing number of specialists from the individual religions and from ethics collaborate in creating or sharpening awareness of a global ethic through shared study of the sources, historical analyses, systematic evaluation and political and social diagnosis;
• That those responsible in all sectors of our society set about involving themselves both theoretically and practically, with all their energies, in this theme of 'an ethic for the world', which is so important for human survival.

I have dedicated this book to Dr Karl Klasen, President Emeritus of the Bundesbank, and his wife Ilse. The friendship of both of them, which now extends over many years, has also become important to me particularly in connection with the theme discussed here. Without my many conversations with Karl and Ilse Klasen, I would not have been able to gain many insights into the real situations in our world. But conversely, both of them have allowed themselves to be challenged by a theologian. As twentieth-century people they found it important to study theological books and then to seek a meeting with their author. That gave rise to a friendship which consists in mutual enrichment and exchange, to the delight of both sides. So I would also like for once to give public expression to my gratitude for much unselfish advice and much friendly encouragement on my way.

A small but efficient team in our Institute for Ecumenical Research has constantly supported me in this academic enterprise, reading the typescript, discussing it and improving it: Karl-Josef Kuschel, Stephan Schlensog and Marianne Saur; technical work on the typescript has been in the hands of Eleonore Henn and Margarite Krause. Stephan Schlensog saw to the design and the graphic representation of my schemes. I am deeply grateful to all of them.

Tübingen, May 1990   Hans Küng

A. No Survival without a World Ethic

Why we need a global ethic

1. From Modernity to Postmodernity

- Every *minute*, the nations of the world spend 1.8 millions of US dollars on military armaments;
- Every *hour*, 1500 children die of hunger-related causes;
- Every *day*, a species becomes extinct;
- Every *week* during the 1980s, more people were detained, tortured, assassinated, made refugee, or in other ways violated by acts of repressive regimes than at any other time in history;
- Every *month*, the world's economic system adds over 7.5 billions of US dollars to the catastrophically unbearable debt burden of more than $1,500 billions now resting on the shoulders of Third World peoples;
- Every *year*, an area of tropical forest three-quarters the size of Korea is destroyed and lost;
- Every *decade*, if present global warming trends continue, the temperature of the earth's atmosphere could rise dramatically (between 1.5 and 4.5 degrees Celsius) with a resultant rise in sea levels that would have disastrous consequences, particularly for coastal areas of all earth's land masses.

In view of these figures,[5] which could easily be supplemented or replaced by similar ones, is there any need for a long explanation of why we need a global ethic to survive? Perhaps not. And yet we cannot spare ourselves the trouble of providing a basis and making the question more specific. For the crisis of the present time is not the result of short-term developments, but the product of crises of long duration. Anyone who raises the question of a global ethic today has to be aware that the present situation is the expression of a far-reaching, epoch-making change which began with the First World War.

1. The Beginning of a Paradigm Shift

In connection with the possibilities of the future a short recollection of the watershed of world history in 1918 is not out of place. History is not very bothered about round numbers in dates. And many historians agree that the nineteenth century only ended with the First World War and the twentieth century only really began in 1918. We can see more clearly that here already there is the beginning of a shift to a new world epoch after the modern period. 'Postmodernity'[6] is a problematic concept, to be sure, and is more an expression of confusion than a definition for a new world epoch which does not yet have a name of its own, but now towards the end of the century people generally are becoming increasingly aware of it.[7] For me, too, postmodernity is neither a magic word nor an omnibus word which explains everything, nor is it a taunt or slogan, but a term which, while open to misunderstanding, is heuristically unavoidable: it is a 'search-term' which needs to be defined more closely and which provides the structure for a problem, the analysis of what distinguishes our epoch from the modern period.

(a) The turning point: 1918

The time of the shift from 'modernity' to 'postmodernity' is usually put too late, making it a sudden development: the tendency is to make the postmodern period begin in the 1970s or 1980s. But the basic onset of modernity already began with the collapse of bourgeois society and the Eurocentric world around the time of the First World War. For Central and Eastern Europe it brought the collapse of the thousand-year old German Reich and the empire of the Tsars, of the four-hundred-year old Protestant state-church system, and of modern liberal theology; along with the downfall of the Hapsburg empire it brought the collapse of the Ottoman Empire and the Chinese Empire. What is decisive is not the word 'postmodernity', which is often used in a nebulous and facile way, but the fact of a global epoch-making upheaval, the implications of which need to be analysed more closely. So I do not want to use the word 'postmodernity', for which a substitute has yet to be found, in a sense which relates primarily to literary history or architectural theory (in which spheres awareness of the problem developed relatively late),[8] but in connection with world history.[9]

Already after the 1914-1918 World War, opportunities also arose to replace with a new, more peaceful, postmodern ordering of the world the shattered world of modernity, which had begun around the middle of the seventeenth century with modern philosophy (Descartes), science (Galileo) and a secular understanding of law, state and politics:

- Already at that time it was clear to many people that the domination of the world by the European powers had already been thoroughly shattered and that after this global political earthquake Eurocentrism would be replaced by a polycentrism (alongside Europe, now America, Soviet Russia and also Japan).
- Already at that time it had become clear to many people that modern science and technology would give wars an essentially different quality of annihilation and that a new world war with a technology of death that had been perfected even further could completely ruin Europe.
- Already at that time there was a peace movement which argued resolutely for total disarmament or even pacifism.
- Already at that time there was a massive criticism of civilization, and far-seeing people had understood that industrialization would not only bring technological progress but in time would also destroy the environment.
- Already at that time the women's movement in many countries had made a definitive breakthrough: equal rights in political elections and in choice of profession began to be established.
- Already at that time, with international conferences and alliances there was a beginning of the ecumenical movement which after the Second World War would lead to the World Council of Churches and the Second Vatican Council.

None of these movements is a 'betrayal' of modernity, born of premodern 'anti-modernist' motivations; all are signs of a productive, forward-looking change towards a new postmodern overall constellation. However, it has to be conceded that at the same time there were also reactionary counter-movements which went the whole way ('totalitarianism').

(b) Catastrophic mistakes

After 1918 the opportunities for a new world order were lost. Why? If we are looking towards the future there is little point in arguing over who was guilty of the catastrophic mistakes of the 1920s and 1930s and speculating what the world would look like today had conquered

Germany not been humiliated in the Treaty of Versailles and Europe and its colonies had been divided up in a different way; had democracy won through instead of Communism, National Socialism and Japanese militarism. In retrospect at any rate, in view of the two world wars, the Gulag archipelago, the Holocaust and the atomic bomb, reasonable people would agree on three things:

- That Fascism in Italy, Spain and Portugal, and National Socialism in Germany - which sparked off the Second World War and the persecution of the Jews - though in modern garb and organized in a modern way, were in the last resort romantic and reactionary nationalist movements which held up the development of a peaceful world order. Through a horrifying war with 55 million dead (including the 6 million Jews murdered in the Holocaust), conquered Europe and then finally also Germany itself were fearfully devastated before the criminal regime collapsed in 1945 in an inferno which it had brought down upon itself.
- That the militarism of Japan (the dominant power in the Far East from the beginning of the century), which was expanding at the same time and suppressing any internal opposition, was a grandiose delusion. While Japan was able to conquer first Korea, Manchuria, areas of China and large parts of South East Asia from Burma through Singapore to New Guinea, in the end it was finally thrown back to its own islands after the dropping of two cruel atomic bombs quickly ended the fighting in 1945.
- That finally even revolutionary Communism, which had only a partial understanding of Karl Marx and his programme, in fact became a reactionary movement. In Russia, a promising democratic movement had begun with the 1917 March Revolution (the deposition of the Tsar). However, the democratic regime was brutally challenged by Lenin after his arrival in April 1917. After Lenin's total defeat in the elections (only 24% of the votes were cast for his Bolsheviks) the first parliament was broken up violently with the help of Red troops in January 1918 and finally a 'dictatorship of the proletariat' was established, in fact the totalitarian dictatorship of the Communist party over the people including the proletariat, with a ban on other parties and any forming of factions. Even Soviet historians nowadays concede that with his politics of violence, lawlessness and mass terror, Lenin became the creator of the first modern totalitarian state, and also seems to have been the inventor

5

of the terrifying concept of the 'concentration camp'. This Leninism became the basis of Stalinism, the so-called 'dictatorship of the proletariat' becoming the presupposition of the Gulag archipelago. A revolution took place here which began in the name of the masses and ended with their impoverishment and enslavement by an enormously privileged and corrupt party hierarchy (the new class of the bureaucratic 'Nomenklatura') - until finally after seven decades, with the arrival in office of Mikhail Gorbachov, the 'man of the decade', in 1985, the ideology of a Communist world revolution was buried and the extremely difficult move towards democracy was begun. Here the free West was of little help.

It is true that all these movements, which in their way sought to overcome the global crisis after the First World War, have proved to have no future. They held up the development of a (relatively!) better world, and after the Second World War for half a century led to a bipolar political, economic and military antagonism between two superpowers (the USA and the USSR) which is now fading. Their slogans could not give the world ethical criteria with which to master the tasks of the future. But what is the position today?

2.Slogans Without a Future

(a) State socialism

Whatever the original justification for Marx's criticism of society and religion may have been and remains,[10] whatever high ideals, like social justice, solidarity, freedom for the oppressed and help for the weak, stood and still stand behind socialism, finally the slogans of the Marxism-Leninism of the socialist state like planned economy, one-party rule, opposition to enmity by a state security apparatus, no longer have a future (and Marxists in all countries cannot get round the fact). The Soviet Union had become a great power only by military means. Hope for justice through a state-controlled distribution organization proved blind to reality, as the decades after the Bolshevik 'October Revolution' in Russia soon showed. The year 1989, in which people in the West were celebrating the French Revolution of 1789, brought the revolution of whole peoples in the East and thus the final collapse of Marxist regimes which had already been regarded as incompetent and

6

corrupt. In 1990 the Communist Party gave up its monopoly of power and a market economy was also introduced (hesitantly) into the Soviet Union.

Let no one deceive themselves: that 'system' of brutal violence, local *apparachiks* and military great-power politics which shed blood in putting down popular rebellions with troops in Berlin in 1953, in Budapest in 1956, in Prague in 1968 and in Gdansk in 1970, in each case following its action with 'normalization', that totalitarian system, will sooner or later also show its lack of a future in China, where as late as 1989 the old-guard Communists dared to take action against the revolutionary power of non-violent masses with tanks.

Neither army nor secret police, nor ideological fixation, total control and bureaucracy, which only result in frustration, resignation, incapacitation and finally radical antipathy to the state, will decide the future of states like the Soviet Union and China, both of which have to solve the scandal of their economies and their long-suppressed problems of nationalism. The future will be decided by an efficient economy in the context of a Soviet confederation (perhaps of smaller dimensions) and a really democratic Chinese republic. It will be decided by a freely developing science, technology and democracy and thus by intellectual freedom, political pluralism and creative initiative. Here, in a region of the world which was previously socialist, there will have to be consideration not only of human rights but also of questions about an ethic, which have been neglected hitherto because they have been 'occupied' by the opposition. Countless people in the Soviet Union and China in particular no longer know what they are working for and what they should live and suffer for. The question therefore is: has capitalism won a victory over socialism, as some people think?

(b) Neocapitalism

Since the First World War, the United States has been the leading power in the Western world in economic, political and military terms, and has won the victory in the bi-polar struggle and the Cold War with the Soviet Union: the spirit of democracy and the ideals of freedom and tolerance have proved stronger than all the brown, red and black dictatorships. North America still has an immense economic, political and also ethical potential.

But even friends of America cannot avoid the insight that the slogans of the neo-capitalists of Wall Street, which one could hear on all sides in the 1980s, have no future, and are proving disastrous for America and its sphere of influence: greed, insatiable avarice, 'Get rich, borrow, spend and enjoy!' Self-enrichment, self-gratification and selfish complacency. The 'Reagan Revolution', also praised as a model by many people in Great Britain and on the European continent, led the United States, the only nation to be a great power in both military and economic terms, to excessive armaments and social retrenchment, and thus at the same time to decline. At the end of the Reagan presidency, which despite all the scandals (like Iran Gate) was staged and 'communicated' in a dazzling way, the United States, which had begun the decade of the 1980s as the greatest creditor nation in the world, stood as the greatest debtor nation, with a low rate of saving and hundreds of billions of dollars of foreign debt - a situation made possible only through gigantic exports on credit, above all from Germany and Japan (great powers only in economic terms). Now this money is not there for investment in Eastern Europe and the Third World.

However, the golden age for expensive hostile takeovers, leveraged buyouts, junk bonds and other forms of activity by the modern robber barons seems to be over. This is because of the two Stock Exchange crashes in the 1980s which were accompanied by the bankruptcy of numerous firms, banks and savings banks, legal proceedings against leading market-makers,[11] and the redundancy of tens of thousands of employees. A blind trust not only in state planning (as in the East) but also in powers of self-regulation in the markets (as in the West) is unfounded: the forces of supply and demand do not necessarily lead to equilibrium; market analysis cannot replace morality. And happily, even in the United States an increasing number of voices are warning against the politics of selfishness, me-ism, yuppie greed and the casino mentality on the stock-market; against the 'conspicuous consumption' of a rich minority and exorbitant special premiums for the elite of American business. In the 1990s, as one could read in *Time* magazine at the beginning of 1990, the bills of the 1980s now have to be paid.[12]

So will being a military atomic 'superpower', which did not do the Soviet Union any good, benefit the USA in the long run? It was economic, social and moral fiasco which undermined the Soviet Union as a superpower. According to the British historian Paul Kennedy,[13] the history of the USA and the USSR seem to confirm the historical experiences of other world powers: rise and hey-day are followed by over-extension, exhaustion and decline. Indeed great historical challenges can sometimes be sustained and overcome by lesser powers, who know what they want and who invest their economic and moral resources accordingly. In view of fading American leadership, financial weaknesses and numerous scandals involving financial corruption, even in the Pentagon, in ministries, federal agencies and Congress, Paul Volcker, the long-standing and respected chairman of the US Federal Reserve, says: 'So, it seems to me, part of keeping America strong and maintaining our leadership will rest on restoring a sense of high ethics and professionalism and challenge in public service itself.'[14] That is the hope of others, that the slow death of covetousness will be followed by a resurrection of integrity.

In truth, now that the old images of hostility have faded and the traditional American national religion of anti-Communism no longer has any basis, there must also be a rethinking among certain American politicians - and not just about armaments: on the one side there are megalomanic projects for armaments and space, and on the other tremendous national deficits in the sectors of public education (primary and secondary schools, illiteracy), social welfare (a growing proletariat), health and environmental protection. The national deficit lies not only in the economic sphere but also in the social, political and moral sphere.

The crisis in the leading great power in the West is, however, a moral crisis of the West generally, including Europe: the destruction of any kind of tradition, of a wider meaning in life, of unconditional ethical criteria, and a lack of new goals, with the resultant psychological damage. Many people nowadays no longer know the basic options according to which they are to make the daily decisions in their life, great or small; the preferences they should follow; the priorities they should establish; the models they should choose. For the authorities and traditions which used to provide tradition are no longer valid. A crisis of orientation is rife, with which the frustration, anxiety, drug and alcohol addiction, Aids, and criminality of many young people have as much to do at one level as the most recent scandals in politics, business, trade unions and society, of which there are all too many even in self-righteous Switzerland, in Germany, Austria, France, Spain and Italy, have to do at another.

In short, the West is faced with a vacuum of meaning, values and

9

norms which is not only a problem for individuals, but also a political issue of the first order. And the decisive question is not whether the West has now finally conquered the socialist East, but whether the West will cope with the immense economic, social, ecological, political and moral problems which it has itself produced. At all events, some rethinking is necessary. But in which direction? In the direction of Japan, which in the Pacific has already replaced the USA as the principal economic power?

(c) 'Japanism'

In the post-war period, despite its devastating defeat, Japan has worked its way to becoming not only the leading industrial power in the Pacific basin but also the third economic world power - after North America and Europe. And yet the very economic efficency which Japan has meanwhile demonstrated to the world so imposingly, and which is so often commended in a very one-sided way to Americans and Europeans by economists as a recipe, seems to be problematical. Nothing is to be said against Japan's efficiency, power of innovation and will to work, at which one can only wonder. But even in Japan itself, where people are working, not without anxiety about setbacks, for an economic (rather than a military) supremacy far beyond the Pacific region, with the help of a large-scale economic and technical offensive, critical voices have been raised since the financial and political scandals at the end of the 1980s and the re-election of corrupt representatives and members of the government during 1990.

Even Japan's wealth and power have limits. And *The Japan That Can Say No* (the title of a bestseller by Akio Morita, the proud president of Sony), which is to take its place as a political great power without any excuses, had to acknowledge with the first crash on the Japanese Stock Exchange at the beginning of 1990 that the rest of the world 'can say no' and refuse to support the yen. Since then the impregnability of the Tokyo stock market is a thing of the past. This should make us look again at efficiency without other considerations, flexibility without principles, authoritarian leadership without responsibility, politics and economics without a moral vision, trade and business without reciprocity, war guilt without consciousness of guilt. In the long run has not all that not only cost Japan the sympathy of other Asian peoples, Europe, and above all the USA, but also undermined Japan's moral foundations, which are important for economic, social, spiritual and cultural survival in the future?

Critical publications, in particular including Karel van Wolferen's *The Enigma of Japanese Power* (1989),[15] may be uncomfortable and one-sided, but they do ask questions about the unconditional, universal validity of certain truths and ethical principles in the social and political reality of Japan. Of course there is a strict and detailed code of behaviour for family and social life in Japan. But is it not true that in social and political life people largely continue to keep at bay the unconditional moral demands of original Buddhism and Confucianism? And that they do so in favour of a Shintoism which sanctions all political deals and social practices; a reverence for nature and ancestors which is only ceremonial, and which has hardly developed any moral doctrines; and in favour of a folkloristic recourse to different religions depending on the time of day and time of life (e.g. Shintoism on a birthday, Christianity at weddings, Buddhism at death)? Here questions arise not only for individuals but for the Japanese system, which is supported by a strong alliance between industry, a highly-qualified bureaucracy and a conservative party in government, for that 'Japanism' as a substitute religion which tacitly regards and treats 'Japan' as the supreme value. And indirectly questions also arise about a 'Christian' Europe or America which may in theory know of an ethic that makes universal and unconditional demands, but in practice very often acts on the basis of a 'situation ethic' which adapts itself pragmatically.

Conversely, can we not understand how many people, particularly in India, Africa and the Arab states, mistrust a total Westernization and for the sake of their cultural identity insist on what is part of their tradition: on an ethic and religion with unconditional validity? Or is the coming world community only to be a community of interests, one gigantic market? And does not the market, of all places, need justice and ethics, as a further dimension and corrective? Should people not reflect in Japan, as well as in Europe, on what modern progress has and has not brought us?

11

3. The End of the Great Modern Ideologies

(a) Criticism of the achievements of the West

In fact there is widespread criticism in Asia and Africa that Western achievements, as they have become established in the modern European world, may have brought the world many great things, but these are not necessarily good:

- Science, but not wisdom to prevent the misuse of scientific research (why not also envisage the industrial production of human material in Japan?);
- Technology, but no spiritual energy to bring the unforeseeable risks of a highly-efficent macrotechnology under control (why not also work on atomic bombs in India and Pakistan instead of combating the mass poverty?);
- Industry, but no ecology, which might fight against the constantly expanding economy (why not cut down tropical rain forest in Brazil by the square kilometre?);
- Democracy, but no morality which could work against the massive interests of various individuals and groups in power (what can one do against the drug cartel in Colombia, the scandal in the Indian Congress Party, the corruption in the Japanese National Liberal Party or the Mobutus in Zaire?).

(b) The demystification of modern ideologies of progress

At the end of the second millennium this is the result of a development in world history in which there is manifestly no determinism with historical 'necessities' à la Hegel, Marx or Spengler, but also no 'end of history', as was prematurely proclaimed; instead, there are constantly new and unexpected shifts and new opennesses. The major modern ideologies which in the past two centuries functioned as 'scientific' total explanations and attractive quasi-religions are on their last legs. And this is not just true of the revolutionary ideology of progress in the Soviet East. There is also a crisis for the evolutionary-technological ideology of progress in the West, which developed in modern times on the basis of a new kind of confidence in reason and a consciousness of freedom, and which beyond question could point to enormous success. Is everything always going to go on like this? Unlimited growth? Endless progress?

In fact eternal, omnipotent, all-gracious progress, that great god of the modern ideologies, with its strict commandments, 'Thou shalt do more and more, better and better, faster and faster', has disclosed that it is fatally two-faced, and belief in progress has lost its credibilty. People have now become generally aware that all over the world economic progress as an end in itself has led to inhuman consequences, often dismissed by scientists as 'side-effects' of scientific progress and by economists as 'external effects' of economic growth. And this happens although these effects are of the first order (even if chronologically they are secondary and tertiary), which result in the destruction of the natural human environment and thus also in large-scale social destabilization. The key words are repeated every day in the media: scarcity of resources, traffic problems, environmental pollution, destruction of the forests, acid rain, greenhouse effect, gap in the ozone layer, climatic change, waste dumping, population explosion, mass unemployment, breakdown of government, international debt crisis, Third World problems, excessive armaments, nuclear winter... The greatest triumphs and greatest catastrophes of technology lie closely together. And one does not have to be a melancholy Cassandra and pestilential killjoy to note that there is a threat that our present society with its concentration on progress will destroy itself.

But the crisis of the idea of progress is essentially the crisis of modern rational understanding. Certainly an enlightened rational criticism of the nobility and the church, state and religion, was an urgent need from the eighteenth century onwards, and it finally also resulted in the self-criticism of reason (Kant's criticisms). But when it increasingly makes itself absolute and compels everything to legitimate itself (along with the freedom of subjectivity), reason, which is not involved in any cosmos and to which nothing is sacred, destroys itself. This analytical reason is nowadays being questioned in a holistic approach, and in turn is being compelled to legitimate itself. The supreme judge of yesterday is becoming today's defendant.[16] Even in the natural sciences, which for a long time regarded the world as a well-oiled machine, since Einstein's general theory of relativity, Heisenberg's quantum mechanics and the discovery of elementary particles, a holistic way of thinking has become established and with it a paradigm change from the classical mechanistic physics of the modern world.[17] Instead of the domination of nature, what Ilya Prigogine[18] calls a 'new covenant' between human beings and nature is becoming urgently necessary.

Here no one can seriously be 'against progress' in principle. What is questionable is just that in large parts of America, Japan and Europe technological and industrial progress has become an absolute value, an idol, in which people believe unconditionally. The decisive issue will be whether technology and industry are still prepared to adapt to human beings, or whether conversely technology and industry create a form of being (if necessary through gene technology) which adapts itself to them. This raises the question: what is the significance of our progress, our science and technology, our economy and society? We shall have to seek the answer beyond the established systems.

(c) Beyond communism and capitalism

For the two typically modern antagonistic social systems, communism (socialism) and capitalism (liberalism), must be regarded as being hopelessly compromised and outdated. In any case these terms have become just empty shells. They have different meanings everywhere and perhaps still exist in their pure form only in totalitarian communist countries like China and Albania, or in particular capitalist countries of South America. In fact classical capitalism has corrected itself by structural elements from socialism, while classical socialism (Marxism) has proved to be uncorrectable. The word 'socialism' (which has always had collectivist connotations) has long been replaced among those with wider horizons by free 'social democracy', and the term 'capitalism' (which always had connotations of individualism and ex-ploitation) by 'social market economy'! So there is a need to work beyond the planned economy and capitalistic market economy (in which the interests of capital enjoy priority and the needs of labour and of nature are neglected) towards a market economy which is socially and ecologically regulated, in which there is a constant attempt to reach a balance between the interests of capital (efficiency, profit) on the one hand and social and ecological interests on the other: in short, an eco-social market economy.

For both Western and Eastern Europe a new consensus seems to be emerging which is already serving as a signal for the rest of the world. Social democracy and social market economy are no longer exclusives, but include each other, so that there is also a need for conservative ('Christian') and liberal parties, each with its own profile. In fact, with the free social state guaranteed by the state, all over the world we are moving towards a mixed system, at any rate if we look more closely: to a new post- capitalist and post-socialist constellation

14

for which the earlier ideologies provide no recipes. However, it is already clear that new dangers are associated with this surprisingly new openness and present a threat.

4. Limit Experiences and Breakthroughs in Innovation

(a) The need for a prophylactic for crises

The following situation cannot be ignored: the pace of technological progress has increased so terrifically that it constantly threatens to overtake political forms. Legislation pursues technological developments with its tongue hanging out, like a hound pursuing its prey. This situation is unsatisfactory, indeed intolerable. Many enthusiastic technological expectations are proving deceptive, and many results ambivalent. So what seems necessary is a forward-looking estimation of the consequences of scientific and technological research, an estimation with a scientific basis which can be translated into practical politics.

Previously, ethics has usually come too late, in so far as it is reflection on the morality of human behaviour. Too often people have asked what we may do only after we have been able to do it. But for the future the decisive thing is that we should know what we may do before we can do it and do indeed do it.[19] Ethics, although it is always conditioned by a particular period and society, should therefore not just be reflection on crises; those who constantly look in the mirror at the way along which they have come will miss the way forward. By means of prognoses of crises which take worst cases into account (as H. Jonas argues), ethics should be a prophylactic for crises. Leading ethicists now agree that we need a preventive ethics. And this should not just begin with industrial production, but already at the stage of experimentation (which has extremely serious consequences in both atomic technology and gene technology), indeed even at the stage of scientific and theoretical reflection, with its priorities and preferences.

(b) Experiences of the limits to what can be done

For it is all too evident that the new millennium will be characterized by extremely dangerous technological limit experiences. New limit experiences, which equally indicate a shift in epochs, can be seen in:

15

1. The use of atomic power, which can be for peaceful or for military ends and which would result in the self-destruction of humankind by a geostrategic blow and counterblow;

2. The development of communication technologies (information technology + telecommunication = telematics), which lead to a gigantic impetus towards excessive information that individuals can no longer cope with because they are completely disorientated;

3. The development of a world stock market, a world money market and a virtually simultaneous world stock exchange which even now can let loose global turbulence in the structure of the currencies and economies of whole continents because it is beyond the control of any authority;

4. The development of gene technology, which through scientific ambition (the 3 billion dollar 'genome project') and unscientific profit motives threatens to lead to monstrous manipulations of human beings and their heredity;

5. The development of medical technology, which raises questions about the implantation and treatment of embryos in accord with human dignity, and also about dying and actively helping people to die in accord with human dignity;

6. The North-South division of the earth: the impoverishment and indebtedness of the Third and Fourth Worlds, which in the 1980s rose from 400 to 1300 billion dollars; we hear that almost 8 million children, mostly in Africa and Latin America, will die in 1990 because of a lack of basic foodstuffs and inoculations.

And yet, precisely as a theologian, my intention here is not to develop a terrifying apocalyptic scenario demonstrating our arrogance about our capabilities and then go on where possible to bring in the Christian religion or even the Christian churches as saviours from all ills. For it is impossible to overlook the positive elements contained specifically in those three modern revolutions which are abiding presuppositions for the breakthroughs into postmodernity.

(c) The post-industrial society

The scientific and technological revolution of the seventeenth century and the socio-political revolution of the eighteenth century (the American and French Revolutions) were followed in the nineteenth century by the industrial revolution. Starting from Great Britain, it embraced all the European and North American states, and also

Japan, and everywhere produced modern industrial society instead of a static agricultural economy. But following this first industrial revolution, which replaced muscle-power with machines and mechanization (steam power, electricity and chemicals), after the Second World War there was a second industrial revolution,[20] which strengthened or replaced human brainpower by machines (through computers and telecommunications). With such innovative technological developments (electronics, miniaturization, digitalization, software), which permeate not only particular areas but the whole of social life, human utopias that once looked fantastic now seem to be being fulfilled.

A postindustrial society is coming into being in postmodernity. By this is to be understood not just a 'leisure society' (to use a term which the American sociologist David Riesman coined as early as the 1950s[21]) but a change in the whole social structure. According to Daniel Bell,[22] it could include the following dimensions, primarily for developed societies:

- In the economy: an increasing predominance of services (the tertiary sector: trade, transport and health, education and training, research and administration) as opposed to productive businesses (primary and secondary sector: agriculture and industry).
- In technology: the central position of theoretical knowledge and the new intellectual technology.
- In social structures: the rise of new technological elites and the transition from a producer society to an information and knowledge society.

Certainly, hitherto all excessively optimistic expectations that a more humane period will come into being automatically have been disappointed: human beings continue to have murderous aggressive and destructive drives, and the dismantling of old antagonisms can and will be followed by the construction of new ones. But pessimistic utopians like O.Spengler, who expected the 'decline of the West' any day, have also been disappointed. Granted, further and great ecological catastrohpes are possible and even probable, but at the same time there are also signs of breakthroughs in innovation which could make survival easier for humanity.[23] The following key innovations should be noted:

1. The conversion of armaments: the redeployment of personnel and technology to civil tasks instead of the production of armaments;

2. Eco-technology: recycling and waste management which respects

17

the environment instead of mountains of waste;

3. Energy-saving technology: solar technology instead of the squandering of fossil fuels;

4. Nuclear fusion: atomic fusion instead of atomic fission;

5. The invention of new materials: environment-friendly instead of environment-hostile materials.

And with innovations in products, social innovations could become established: structures of partnership, new forms of the active integration say of older people into education, business and politics. All in all, given the acceleration in the dynamics of the world economy, a breakthrough seems possible to an ecological economy which is more orientated on peace. Or are all these only illusions?

(d) The postmodern break-through

1989, the very year of the Great European Revolution, gave encouragement and hope to many people. For the first time since the Second World War, there seem to be concrete possibilities of a world which is not only without war, but also peaceful and cooperative. Despite all the old tensions and new ethnic and religious antagonisms, despite all the possible conflicts and setbacks, the possibility of global collaboration in the interest of progress for all no longer seems to be an unrealistic vision. For,

- Militarism seems to be fading into the background; the period of the Cold War between East and West and with it also the intermediate phase of the domination of two superpowers seems to be over; politically, the East-West situation is more favourable than at any time since the Second World War;
- Billions of dollars, roubles, marks, francs and pounds which are now becoming free as a result of the radical reduction of military establishments could be diverted to the civil sector;[24]
- For the first time since the end of the Second World War the lands of the Eastern bloc are getting the opportunity to link up with the development of the West and slowly raise their own economic level, with the aim of mass prosperity;
- The West - America and the Europe that is growing together - is getting the opportunity finally to implement *perestroika* in its own sphere, above all in connection with agriculture, social policy and homebuilding, protectionist trade policies and national deficits;

18

- Powers being released from the East-West crisis could finally be diverted to overcome not only the social and economic north-south crisis but also the global ecological crisis.

There is no trace of an 'end of history' - as constantly conjectured in Hegel's 'philosophy of art', in Alexandre Kojève's Hegel studies or in the political speculation of the American Francis Fukuyama! That makes all the more urgent the question: what aims are meaningful, what values capable of achieving a consensus, what convictions justifiable? This is a question not only for social scientists, philosophers and theologians but for anyone, man or woman, old or young, who takes an active part in the course of this world. Here it is not just a question of individual goals, values and convictions, nor even simply of 'Megatrends 2000', superficially extrapolated and optimistically added together, which are to culminate in the 'end of the welfare state' (Thatcherism) and in the 'triumph of the individual'.[25] Here - particularly in view of the change in civilization which is accelerating as steadily as ever - it is a question of a fundamental and long-term change in the world order which has to be assessed realistically: a new basic orientation, a new macroparadigm, a new overall postmodern constellation.[26] I shall now attempt to give a summary description of it.

5. The Rising World Constellation of Postmodernity

(a) Dimensions of the overall constellation of postmodernity

We saw that already since the two world wars humankind has been caught up in an epoch-making paradigm-shift from modernity to postmodernity, in a change of overall constellation which has now also broken through into mass consciousness. At present we still do not even know what our new age will be called, what names (like 'Reformation', 'Enlightenment') or nicknames ('baroque', 'rococo') will be given to it. However, the substitute term 'postmodern' can already be replaced by some positive definitions. Increasingly more clearly - despite all counter-movements, deviant trends and crises that are to be expected - the postmodern world constellation, to put it briefly, shows the following dimensions:
- Geopolitically, we have a post-Eurocentric constellation: the domination of the world by five rival European national states (England,

19

France, Austria, Prussia/Germany and Russia) is over. Today we are confronted with a polycentric constellation of different regions of the world, with North America, Soviet Russia, the European community in the lead, and later probably also China and India.

- Foreign policy has to reckon with a post-colonial and post-imperialist world society. Specifically (in the ideal case) this means nations which cooperate internationally and are truly united.
- Economic policy has to reckon with the development of a post-capitalist, post-socialist economy. With some justification it can be called an eco-social market economy.
- Social policy has to recognize the increasing formation of a post-capitalist, post-socialist society. In the developed countries it will be increasingly a society dominated by service industries and communication.
- Those concerned with sexual equality see the appearance of a post-patriarchal society. In family, professional, and public life a relationship is clearly developing between men and women which is more a partnership.
- Culturally, we are moving in the direction of a post-ideological culture. In future it will be a culture more orientated on an overall plurality.
- In religious terms, a post-confessional and inter-religious world is coming into being. In other words, slowly and laboriously a multi-confessional ecumenical world society is coming into being.

This epoch-making paradigm shift which covers the world in which we live, our working world, the cultural world, and the world of the state, is concerned not least with new values. But precisely at this point an approach which is pessimistic about culture can easily miss the essentials.

(b) Not a destruction of values but a change of values

The paradigm shift does not necessary include a destruction of values, but rather a fundamental shift in values:[27]
- From an ethic-free society to an ethically responsible society;
- From a technocracy which dominates people to a technology which serves the humanity of men and women;
- From an industry which destroys the environment to an industry which furthers the true interests and needs of men and women in

20

accord with nature;

- From the legal form of a democracy to a democracy which is lived out and in which freedom and justice are reconciled.

It also follows that this is a social shift not against, averse to, science, technology, industry and democracy, but a shift with, in alliance with, these social powers which formerly were absolutized but have now been relativized. The specific values of industrial modernity - diligence *(industria!)*, rationality, order, thoroughness, punctuality, sobriety, achievement, efficiency - are not just to be done away with but to be reinterpreted in a new constellation and combined with the new values of postmodernity: with imagination, sensitivity, emotion, warmth, tenderness, humanity. So it is not a matter of repudiations and condemnations, but of counterbalances, counter-plans, counter-directions and counter-movements.

(c) A holistic view

From the changes in physics through the alternative methods of homeopathic medicine to humanistic psychology and the new awareness of the environment, nowadays an intensified holistic way of thinking can be seen which could also make possible a balance between the European-American and the Asiatic way of thinking.[28] At any rate, what is required today - and here there may be agreement between the most rationalistic systematic theoreticians (like N.Luhmann) and hermeneutical philosophers (like G.Gadamer), through serious researchers into the future (like R.Jungk, E.Laszlo) to the pioneers of the New Age (like F.Capra) - is an equilibrium between the rational tendencies and the emotional and aesthetic tendencies of human beings, indeed a holistic view of the world and human beings in their different dimensions. For along with the economic, social and political dimension there is also the aesthetic, ethical and religious dimension of human beings and humanity.

Human society is also multi-dimensional, and nowadays we must adjust to complex, interwoven and dynamic inter-relationships. And if in view of all the trends and tendencies towards 'globalization' or 'homologization' (world-wide standardization, from eating and drinking habits through fashions and media to concrete structures), counter-trends and counter-tendencies in the direction of cultural, linguistic and religious self- assertion manifest themselves, these may not be

21

dismissed *a priori* as cultural nationalism, linguistic chauvinism and religious traditionalism.

What should become clear from these remarks is that it is not my concern to opt for a new unitary ideology, to present the new global outline of a social utopia. What is important, rather, is soberly and modestly to seek a way into the future from the needs and distresses of the modern age: a postmodern way. I think that I have already set the markers clearly enough to right and left and can sum them up here.

(d) Not contra-modernity, not ultra-modernity, but taking modernity up into what transcends and replaces it

Postmodernity in the sense that I have described cannot be content with a radical pluralism or relativism ('truth, justice, humanity in the plural', to refer to J.-F.Lyotard[29] and W.Welsch[30]), which in fact are characteristics of the disintegration of late modernity. Randomness, colourfulness, the mixing-up of all and everything, the anarchy of trends of thought and styles, the methodological 'anything goes', the moral 'all is permissible': this and similar phenomena cannot be the signature of the postmodern period. To this degree conservative criticism of modernity (like that of R.Spaemann)[31] is quite justified.

However, postmodernity cannot aim at a uniform interpretation of the world in which we live. Nor can wholeness in the sense of totality and integrity and some premodern church integralism, or a 'postmodern classicism in architecture', or an 'essentialism or "Neoaristotelianism" in philosophy',[32] be hallmarks of the postmodern period either. Even within the new paradigm there will be a multiplicity of heterogeneous options for living, patterns of action, language games, forms of life, scientific conceptions, economic systems, social models and communities of faith, but these do not rule out a fundamental social consensus.

Postmodernity as developed here means neither just romanticizing cosmetic operations in architecture or society nor a theory which is a panacea for social, economic, political, cultural or religious organization. Postmodernity in the sense developed above strives for a new basic consensus of integrative humane convictions in a new world constellation towards which democratic pluralistic society is inexorably directed if it is to survive. In principle, this means:

22

1. Postmodernity does not mean anti-modernity! A sweeping anti-modernism in the religions, orientated on the past, is no contribution to overcoming our epoch-making crisis. Here is no conservative prejudice for the old. Any form of programmatic anti-Enlightenment and church conservatism is to be rejected. A 'renewed Christian Europe' in the premodern sense in which those who believe otherwise or do not believe at all are in fact excluded is a clerical delusion. And much as a spiritual renewal of Europe is necessary, one form of it may be doomed to failure from the start. That is the backward-looking utopia of a 'spiritual unity of Europe' in which the confessional walls between Catholics, Protestants and Orthodox are retained, leading to the restoration programme of a 're-evangelization of Europe' in a Roman Catholic direction which John Paul II proclaimed in 1982 in the mediaeval pilgrimage centre of Santiago di Compostela and again in 1990 in Prague (at the same time insisting on the need for obedience to the church). For such a programme is acompanied by a constant denunciation of Western democracy as consumerism, hedonism and materialism, not by an unambiguous affirmation of the modern values of freedom, pluralism and tolerance - right into the sphere of the Pope's own church (questions of birth control and sexual morality!).[33] And are Christians self-righteously going to criticize Islam (for a theocratic conception of the state, the exclusion of women from public life, rigorous sexual morality and xenophobia)? To put it bluntly: no regressive or repressive religion - whether Christian, Islamic, Jewish or of whatever provenance - has a long-term future.[34]

2. But postmodern does not mean ultra-modern either! An apologetic modernism with a fixation on the present is likewise no contribution towards the solution of the epoch-making crisis. There can be no progressive prejudice for the new. A simple heightening, potentiation and modernization of modernity - postmodernity as a philosophical development and consummation of modernity - does not take the break in epochs seriously. Modernism too can become traditionalism. So here, too, the mere reproduction and continuation of the Enlightenment can fail. Reason cannot simply be rehabilitated by reason, nor can the basic defects of science and the great damage done by technology simply be removed by yet more science and yet more technology, as many people of action in economics and politics think, in a remarkable coalition with the 'intractable supporters of the Enlightenment'.

Natural science and technology can displace a past ethic, but they cannot themselves produce a new ethic or even provide the justification for it.

3. If the epoch-making paradigm shift can be compressed into one term, the modern paradigm must be 'sublated' into modernity in Hegel's threefold term. Modernity is:
- to be affirmed in its humane content,
- to be denied in its inhuman limits, and
- to be transcended in a new, differentiated, pluralistic and holistic synthesis.

I have pointed to the various dimensions of this new synthesis ('the postmodern constellation'). Now I shall make them more specific by indicating some basic convictions and demands in the direction of a world ethic.[35]

II. Why Ethics?

It should have become clear that, at least on negative grounds, the catastrophic economic, social, political and ecological developments of both the first and the second halves of the century necessitate a world ethic if humankind is to survive on this earth. Diagnoses of disaster have been of little help to us here.[36] Nor might a pragmatic social technology without foundations for values, of a Western or Eastern tendency, be enough.[37] But without morality, without universally binding ethical norms, indeed without 'global standards', the nations are in danger of manoeuvring themselves into a crisis which can ultimately lead to national collapse, i.e. to economic ruin, social disintegration and political catastrophe.

In other words, we need reflection on ethics, on the basic moral attitude of human beings; we need an ethical system, a philosophical or theological theory of values and norms, to direct our decisions and actions. The crisis must be seen as an opportunity, and a 'response' must be found to the 'challenge'. But an answer in negative terms can hardly be enough if ethics is not to degenerate into a technique for repairing[38] defects and weaknesses. So we must take the trouble to give a positive answer to the question of a world ethic. We begin with the basic question of any ethics. Why ethics at all? Why be moral?

1. Beyond Good and Evil?

(a) Why not do evil?

Why should people do good and not evil? Why are not human beings 'beyond good and evil' (F. Nietzsche) and only obligated to their 'will to power' (success, riches and contentment)? Elementary questions are often the most difficult of all - and such questions no longer arise just for the 'permissive' West. Much - morals, laws and customs - that was taken for granted down the centuries because it was supported by religious authority is no longer taken for granted nowadays all over the world. Questions like these occur to every individual:

- Why should human beings not lie to, deceive, rob their fellows if this is to their advantage and in any particular instance one does not have to fear discovery and punishment?
- Why should the politician resist corruption if he can be sure of the discretion of the one who offers the bribe?
- Why should a businessman (or a bank) set a limit to the profit motive, if greed, if the slogan 'get rich', is preached publicly without any moral constraints?
- Why should someone engaged in embryo research (or a research institute) not develop a commercial technique for implantation which guarantees the production of flawless embryos and throws the surplus on the rubbish heap?
- Why should unwanted (say, female) offspring whose sex has been determined before birth not be liquidated right away?

But the questions are also addressed to the great collectives. Why may a people, a race, a religion, not hate, harass and, if that is its concern, even exile or liquidate a minority of another kind, another faith, or even one that is 'foreign'?

But enough of negatives!

(b) Why do good?

Here, too, questions arise first for the individual:
- Why should people be friendly, compassionate and even ready to help instead of being heedless and brutal; why should a young person renounce the use of force and in principle opt for non-violence?
- Why should a businessman (or a bank) behave with absolute correctness even when there are no controls? Why should a trade union official fight not only for an organization but also for the common good, even if it damages his or her own career?
- Why should human beings never be the object of commercialization and industrialization (the embryo as a marketable article and an object of trade) for scientists, doctors involved in implantation and their institutes, but always be legal subjects and goals of the process?

But here too questions are addressed to the great collectives:
- Why should one people show tolerance, respect and even appreciation to another?
- Why should one race show these to another?

26

- Why should one religion show these to another?
- Why should those in authority in the nations and religions in all circumstances commit themselves to peace and never to war?

So to put the basic question once again: why should human beings - understood as individuals, groups, nations or religions - act in a human, truly human way? And why should they do this unconditionally - that is, in every case? And why should they all do this, and no class, clique or group be excepted? That is the basic question for every ethics.

2. No Democracy without Basic Consensus

(a) The dilemma of democracy

It may be evident that here we have a basic problem of Western democracy about which we are not to moralize in a self-righteous way but on which we are to reflect self-critically. For on the basis of its self-understanding the free democratic state - in contrast to the mediaeval clerical ('black') state or the modern totalitarian ('brown' or 'red') state - must be neutral in its world-view. That means that it must tolerate different religions and confessions, philosophies and ideologies. And beyond question this represents tremendous progress in the history of humankind, with the result that nowadays, all over the world, there is tremendous longing for freedom and human rights which no Western intellectual who constantly enjoys Western freedom should disavow as 'typically Western'. Given its constitution, the democratic state must observe, protect and further freedom of conscience and religion, freedom of the press and of assembly, and everything that is counted among modern human rights. Nevertheless, in all this the state may not decree any interpretation of life or lifestyle; it may not prescribe any supreme values and ultimate norms by law, if it is not to violate the neutrality of its world-view.

Here, obviously, is the basis of the dilemma of any modern democratic state (whether in Europe, America, India or Japan): it has to take into account precisely that which it may not prescribe by law. If the different world-views within it are to live together, the pluralistic society in particular needs a basic consensus to which these worldviews contribute, to bring about the formation of a consensus which is

27

not 'strict' or total, but 'overlapping' (John Rawls[39]). How far this 'overlapping' basic ethical consensus must go in particular instances depends on the historical situation. Thus for a long time people did not have to worry, say, about the preservation and protection of non-human nature, which nowadays is important for survival. So the consensus must constantly be found afresh in a dynamic process.[40]

(b) A minimum of common values, norms and attitudes

Nowadays there is largely agreement here. Without a minimal basic consensus on certain values, norms and attitudes, no human society worth living in is possible in either a smaller or a larger community. Even a modern democracy cannot function without such a basic consensus, which constantly has to be rediscovered in dialogue; indeed it collapses into chaos or a dictatorship - as was shown, say, by the Weimar republic between 1919 and 1933.

What does a minimal basic consensus mean? I shall clarify this on a few points:

- What is the presupposition of internal peace in a smaller or larger community? An agreement that social conflicts will be solved without violence.
- What is the presupposition of economic and legal order? An agreement that a particular order and laws will be obeyed.
- What is the presupposition for institutions which support this order and yet are subject to constant historical change? The will at least to go on giving them tacit assent.

But it is a fact that conversely, in the ideological controversies of a technological world which has become abstract and impossible to survey, in some places the reaction is always one of terror that there will be even more acceptance of Machiavellianism in politics, sharkish methods in the stock market and libertinism in private life. Once again, what we need here is not moralizing, but reflection.

(c) Freely chosen ties

If modern society is to function, the question of the aims and the 'ligatures' (to use Ralf Dahrendorf's phrase), the freely chosen bonds of the individual, may not be neglected. These ties may not become

28

fetters and chains for men and women, but must be help and support. And fundamental to human life is a commitment to a direction in life, to values, to norms, to attitudes, to a meaning in life: one which - unless everything is deceptive - is transnational and transcultural.

People are normally conscious of the ineradicable longing to hold on to something, to rely on something: to have a standpoint in the bewilderingly complex technolological world and in the errors and confusions of their private life, to follow some guideline, to have some standards, to have a goal. In short, people feel the longing to possess something like a basic ethical orientation. And though communication open on all sides, which is stressed so much by social psychology, is doubtless important in a modern society made uncertain by excessive information and disinformation; although the model of an 'alternative dispute resolution'[41] which has been proposed for legal practice is doubtless also important legally, without any ties to meaning, values and norms people will not be able to act in a truly human way in matters large or small.

But what could be the maxims for the future in this context? What would be the ethical goal for the third millennium? What would be the slogan for a strategy of the future?

The key concept for our strategy for the future must be: human responsibility for this planet, a planetary responsibility.

3. The Slogan of the Future: Planetary Responsibility

(a) An ethic of responsibility in place of an ethic of success or disposition

Calling for global responsibility is first and foremost the opposite of calling for what is a mere ethic of success: it is the opposite of an action for which the end sanctifies the means and for which whatever functions, brings profit, power or enjoyment, is good. This in particular can lead to crass libertinism and Machiavellianism. Such an ethic can have no future.

Nor, however, can a mere dispositional ethics have a future either. Orientated on an idea of value seen more or less in isolation (justice, love, truth), it is concerned only with the purely inner motivation of the agent, without bothering about the consequences of a decision or an action, with the concrete situation, its demands and effects. Such

29

an 'absolute' ethic is unhistorical in a dangerous way (it ignores the complexity of the historical situation as it has developed); it is unpolitical (it ignores the complexity of the given social structures and power-relationships); but precisely in this respect, if need be it can justify even terrorism on grounds of disposition.

By contrast, an ethics of responsibility, of the kind that the great sociologist Max Weber proposed in the revolutionary winter of 1918/19, might have some future. Even according to Weber, such an ethic is not 'without a disposition'; however, it always asks realistically about the foreseeable 'consequences' of our action and takes responsibility for them: 'to this degree a dispositional ethics and an ethics of responsibility are not absolute opposites, but supplement each other; it takes both of them to make the authentic person who can have the "call to politics".'[42] Without a dispositional ethics, the ethics of responsibility would decline into an ethics of success regardless of disposition, for which the end justifies any means. Without an ethics of responsibility, dispositional ethics would decline into the fostering of self-righteous inwardness.

Since the First World War, however, human knowledge and power have grown immeasurably - with extremely dangerous long-term consequences for the generations to come. This is demonstrated to us particularly in the spheres of nuclear energy and gene technology. At the end of the 1970s the German-American philosopher Hans Jonas[43] therefore thought through 'the principle of responsibility' in a completely changed world situation in a new and comprehensive way for our technological civilization, in the light of the danger to the ongoing existence of the human species. This involves action in global responsibility for the whole of the biosphere, lithosphere, hydrosphere and atmosphere of our planet. And this includes a self-imposed limitation by human beings on their freedom in the present for the sake of their survival in the future - one need think only of the energy crisis, the exhaustion of natural resources and population growth. So a new kind of ethic is called for out of concern for the future (which makes people wise) and reverence for nature.

(b) Responsibility for our neighbours, the environment and the world after us

So in concrete terms, the slogan for the third millennium should run: world society is responsible for its own future! This is responsibility for

30

our society and environment and also for the world after us. Those responsible in the various regions, religions and ideologies of the world are called on to learn to think and act in a global context.[44] Here there are certainly particular demands on three regions of the world which are economic leaders: the European community, North America and the Pacific area. They also have a responsibility which they cannot get rid of, for the development of other regions of the world: Eastern Europe, Latin America, Southern Asia and Africa - where now, after the encouraging developments in Eastern Europe, one also longs for positive changes.

So on the threshold of the third millennium the cardinal ethical question is raised all the more urgently. On what basic conditions can we survive, survive as human beings, on a habitable earth, and give human form to our individual and social life? On what presuppositions can human civilization be rescued for the third millennium? What basic principles should be followed by the leading forces in politics, economics, science and the religions? And on what basis can the individual, too, achieve a happy and fulfilled existence?

(c) Human beings: the goal and criterion

The answer is that human beings must become more than they are; they must become more human! What is good for human beings is what preserves and furthers their humanity and makes it succeed - and does so in quite a different way from before. Human beings must exhaust their human potential in an unprecedented way to produce the most humane society possible and an intact environment. For the possibilities of humanity that they can activate are greater than the *status quo*. To this extent the realistic principle of responsibility and the 'utopian' principle of hope (Ernst Bloch) belong together.

So there is nothing against the present-day 'self-tendencies' (self-determination, experience of self, self-discovery, self-realization, self-fulfilment) - as long as they are not detached from responsibility for oneself and the world, from responsibility for our fellow human beings, for society and nature; as long as they do not deteriorate into narcissistic reflection on and autistic relationship to the self. Self-assertion and unselfishness need not be mutually exclusive. Identity and solidarity are both required for the formation of a better world.

But whatever projects one plans for a better human future, the basic

31

ethical principle must be that human beings may never be made mere means. They must remain an ultimate end, and always be a goal and criterion - since Kant that has been a way of formulating the categorical imperative. Money and capital are means, as work is a means. Science, technology and industry are also means. They too are in no way 'value-free', 'neutral', but in each individual case have to be assessed and used in terms of the degree to which they serve human development. For example, manipulation of genes in human gametes is therefore legitimate only to the degree that it serves the protection, preservation and humanization of human life; research which uses up the embryo is a human experiment which is to be strictly repudiated as being inhumane.

And as for business: I once heard the American management guru Professor Peter Drucker, who recently has announced the replacement of the 'business society' by the 'knowledge society', in which education and training would have a key position,[45] remark that 'Profit is not a goal but a result'. But we already know now that computers and machines too, cybernetics and management, organization and system are there for human beings and not vice versa. In other words: human beings must always remain the subject and never become the object. What holds for politics on a large scale also applies in the everyday handling of business (as economic psychologists and business specialists are also telling us): 'The "human factor" is the central driving force or restraining element in business and in global events' (Roland Müller).[46] Or as Knut Bleicher puts it in a comparison of management analysis in different cultures (USA - Europe - Japan): 'It is not machines which produce inventions and innovations, but people who are motivated to set their intellect to recognizing opportunities, avoiding risks and creating new economic, social and technological conditions through their activities. Instead of material capital which was decisive for the success of businesses in times of stable developments, it is now human capital that determines the future success of a business.'[47] Humankind will not be saved by the computer but by human beings.

(d) Ethics as public concern

Hence we can recognize as a programmatic demand that ethics, which in modern times has increasingly been regarded as a private matter, must again become a public concern of prime importance in postmod-

32

ernity - for human wellbeing and for the survival of humankind. Here it is not enough to employ ethical experts in the various social institutions in individual cases. In view of the tremendous complexity of the problems and the specialization of science and technology, ethics itself needs to be institutionalized. It has already progressed further in this direction in North America than in Europe and Japan: ethical commissions, chairs in ethics and codes of ethics have been created, especially in the spheres of biology, medicine, technology and economy (e.g. a code of business ethics which, for example, resolutely attacks increasing corruption).[48]

It should not be forgotten that economic thought and action, too, are not value-free or value-neutral. For example the view that it is the exclusive concern of a business to make a profit and that the maximization of profit is the best and only contribution of a business to the prosperity of a society is increasingly being regarded as an outdated standpoint, even among economists and business specialists. Economists, too, are reflecting nowadays on the fact that the great European theoreticians on economics and society from Aristotle and Plato through Thomas Aquinas to the moral philosopher Adam Smith, the founder of modern economics, have seen economics and politics in an overall ethical context.

But those who act ethically do not therefore act in an unbusinesslike way; they take precautions against crises. Some major firms have had to suffer serious losses before learning that the most successful business economically is not the one which has no concern for the ecological, political or ethical implications of its products, but the one which takes these into account - possibly making short-term sacrifices - and so from the start avoids painful penalties and legal restrictions.[49]

Just as the social and ecological responsibility of business cannot simply be foisted on to politicians, so moral and ethical responsibility cannot simply be foisted on to religion. There are businessmen who are even asked at the dinner table by their critical sons and daughters whether such a split between economics and morality, between a purely profit-orientated business at work and ethical private life at home is still credible. No, ethical action should not be just a private addition to marketing plans, sales strategies, ecological bookkeeping and social balance-sheets, but should form the natural framework for human social action. For even the market economy, if it is to function socially and be regulated ecologically, needs people who are supported

33

by very definite convictions and attitudes. Indeed, in general it may be said:

(e) No ordering of the world without a world ethic

For one thing is certain: human beings cannot be improved by more and more laws and regulations, nor can they be improved simply by psychology and sociology. In matters great and small people are confronted with the same situation: knowing about things is not the same as knowing about meanings; regulations are not in themselves orientations, nor are laws morals. Even the law needs a moral foundation! The ethical acceptance of the laws (which the state provides with sanctions and can impose by force) is the presupposition of any political culture. What is the use of more and more laws to individual states or organizations, whether these are the European Community, the United States of America or the United Nations, if a majority of people has no intention of keeping them and constantly finds enough ways and means of irresponsibly imposing their own or collective interests? In the next five years, for example, because of the new drug wave, the US National Council on Crime and Delinquency estimates that new cells must be built for 460,000 new prisoners and in all 35 billion dollars must be spent.[50] On economic grounds alone, therefore, the demand for more supervision, police, prisons and stronger laws cannot be the only solution for coping with such difficult problems of our time. In addition to the question of the financing of a replacement for the cocaine plantations in South America there is obviously also a basic educational problem (in the family, in schools, in groups and in the public) in North America and in Europe. *Quid leges sine moribus* runs a Roman saying: What is the use of laws without morals?

Certainly all the states of the world have an economic and legal order, but this will not function in any state in the world without an ethical consensus, an ethic of its citizens on the basis of which democratic constitutions can function. Certainly the international community of states has also created trans-national, trans-cultural and trans-religious legal structures (without which international treaties would be sheer self-deception); but what is a world order without a binding and obligatory ethic for the whole of humankind - for all its time- conditioned nature - i.e. without a world ethic? Not least, the world market calls for a world ethic. The world economy can less than ever tolerate areas with utterly different ethics or even ethics which are contradictory on central points. What is the use of prohibitions with an ethical foundation in one country (one thinks of particular manipulations of finances or the stock market, or of aggressive research into gene technology) if they can be got round by going to other countries? If ethics is to function for the wellbeing of all, it must be indivisible. The undivided world increasingly needs an undivided ethic. Postmodern men and women need common values, goals, ideals, visions. But the great question in dispute is: does not all this presuppose a religious faith?

III. A Coalition of Believers and Non-Believers

There is no disputing the fact that over the millennia the religions were the systems of orientation which formed the foundation for a particular morality, which legitimated it, motivated it and often also sanctioned punishments. But does that need to be the case even now, in our largely secularized society?

1. Why not Morality without Religion?

(a) Religions: ambivalent phenomena

No one can deny the fact that religions, like all historical entities which have been ambivalent for men and women, have perceived their moral function for better and for worse. For better and for worse: only the prejudiced can fail to concede that the high religions in particular have contributed a great deal to the spiritual and moral progress of the peoples. But it is equally impossible to deny that they have also often hindered, and indeed prevented, this progress. The religions have often less proved to be the motive forces of progress (which was the case with the Protestant Reformation, for all its one-sidedness and weaknesses), than presented themselves as bastions of counter-reform and counter-enlightenment (this already happened in the sixteenth and nineteenth centuries and is doing so again in autocratic, power-obsessed Vatican Rome).

Both positive and negative elements can be reported not only of Christianity but also of Judaism and Islam, Hinduism and Buddhism, Chinese Confucianism and Taoism. In each of the great world religions, in addition to a more or less triumphal history of success (which is usually better known to the adherents) there is also a chronicle of scandal (which they prefer to keep quiet about). Down to our day there are times when, as the American psychiatrist Edgar Draper put it, 'institutionalized religion was not particularly disturbed about its bi-

36

zarre adherents, wild tendencies, comic saints, lascivious Brahmans, paranoid preachers, disturbed rabbis, eccentric bishops or psychopathic popes; it still seemed ready to concede strength of character to such heretics, reformers or rebels who opposed its teaching.'[51] Consequently many people ask even more: why not morality without religion?

(b) Cannot people also live moral lives without religion?

Even believers would have to concede that a moral life is possible without religion.[52] To what extent?

1. Biographically and psychologically there are sufficient reasons why enlightened contemporaries want to renounce religion which had deteriorated into obscurantism, superstition, stultification and 'opium' of the people.

2. Empirically it is indisputable that non-religious people in fact have a basic ethical orientation and lead a moral life even without religion, indeed that in history there have often been religious non-believers who pioneered a new sense of human worth and did more for adulthood, freedom of conscience, freedom of religion and other human rights than their religious allies.

3. Anthropologically, it cannot be denied that many non-religious people in principle have also developed and possess goals and priorities, values and norms, ideals and models, criteria for truth and falsehood.

4. Philosophically, there is no denying that men and women as rational beings have a real human autonomy which allows them to have a basic trust in reality even without belief in God, and leads them to perceive their responsibility in the world: a responsibility for themselves and the world.[53]

(c) Freedom to decide for or against religion

So it is beyond dispute that many secular people nowadays are pioneering a morality which takes its bearings from the human dignity of all men and women, and according to present understanding this human dignity includes reason and responsibility, freedom of conscience, freedom of religion and the other human rights which have become established over the course of a long history - often enough laboriously over against the established religions. And it is of the utmost significance for peace among the peoples, for international collaboration in politics, economics and culture, and also for international organizations like UNO and UNESCO, that religious people - whether they are Jews, Christians or Muslims, Hindus, Sikhs, Buddhists, Confucians, Taoists or whatever - concede to non- religious people, who call themselves 'humanists' or 'Marxists', that they too can in their own way advocate and defend human dignity and human rights, in short a humane ethic. In fact both believers and unbelievers advocate what stands as article 1 in the United Nations Declaration of Human Rights which was passed on 10 December 1948 - after the Second World War and the Holocaust: 'All human beings are born free and equal in dignity and rights. They are endowed with reason and conscience and should act towards one another in a spirit of brotherhood.'

Hence, too, the right to freedom of religion, in a twofold sense - which fanatical believers are all too ready to suppress: freedom for religion on the one hand but freedom from religion on the other. So the right to freedom consistently also includes the right to having no religion: 'Everyone has the right to freedom of thought, conscience and religion; this right includes freedom to change his religion or belief, and freedom, either alone or in community with others and in public and in private, to manifest his religion or belief in teaching, practice, worship and observance' (Article 18).

All this, it seems, can easily be grounded in human reason alone without any principles of belief. So why should not human beings, as Immanuel Kant requires in his programmatic writing 'What is Enlightenment?', overcome the 'tutelage to which they have submitted themselves', the 'inability to make use of their understanding without direction from someone else', and also use their understanding as the foundation of an ethics of reason? According to Kant this inability does not lie in a 'lack of understanding but of courage': 'Have the courage to make use of your own understanding!' Hence today, too, many philosophical and theological ethicists advocate and defend an authentic human autonomy in all practical human decisions, a moral autonomy which even Christian faith cannot simply do away with. Mutual respect - at the least - is called for, mutual respect of believers and non-believers.

2. Shared Responsibility with Mutual Respect

(a) The need for a coalition

However, a coalition of believers and non-believers (deists, atheists, agnostics) in mutual respect may also be necessary for a common world ethic. Why? I have already developed this basic notion and here can simply sum it up once again.

1. The danger of a vacuum of meaning, values and norms threatens both believers and unbelievers. Together we must counter the loss of the old traditions and authorities which provided orientation and the quite fatal crisis in orientation which ensues.

2. A democracy without a prelegal consensus finds itself in difficulties over legitimation. Certainly the free democratic state must be neutral in its world-view, but it needs a minimal basic consensus in respect of particular values, norms and attitudes, because without this basic moral consensus a society worth living in is impossible. It follows from this that:

3. There can be no survival for human society without ethics; to be specific, there can be no internal peace without an agreement to solve social conflicts without violence.

There can be no economic or legal order without the will to observe a particular order and particular laws.

There can be no institutions without at least the tacit consent of the citizens concerned.

(b) The possibility of achieving a coalition

However, if such a coalition between believers and non-believers is necessary in the interest of a world ethic, can it be realized in practice? Yes, because non-believers can join believers in resisting all trivial nihilism, diffused cynicism and social apathy and devote themselves with conviction to making sure that:

1. The basic right of all human beings to a life worth living (no matter what sex, nation, religion, race or class they belong to) is not largely ignored, as it used to be, but is increasingly being realized;

2. In contrast to the 1980s, which were largely lost in this respect, the gap between rich and poor countries does not become any greater;

3. The slums in the poorest areas of the Fourth World do not grow any further;

4. The level of prosperity achieved is not spoiled by ecological

39

catastrophes and international migrations;

5. A world society without war becomes possible in which the material imbalances are slowly remedied by raising the standard of living of the poorer people.

If the revival of traditional oppositions (conservative-liberal, clerical-lay. . .) is to be avoided, above all in the new Europe, which in no way can again be a pre-modern 'Christian' Europe, great importance must be attached to a coalition between believers and non-believers. However, such a coalition is not free from intrinsic problems.

IV. Ethics in Tension between Autonomy and Religion

If a coalition between believers and non-believers is necessary and politically opportune, the counter-question arises: 'From where do we get those criteria which are to guide us and, if necessary, put us in our place? Science cannot teach us such norms.' Thus a prominent scientist, Hubert Markl, a biologist specializing in evolution who is President of the German Society for Research. He warns us not only against an anti-scientific fundamentalism, but also against a 'value-free' science, which no longer tells us 'why we should know what it teaches us'.[54]

1. Rational Difficulties with Ethics

(a) The dialectic of the Enlightenment

The undisputed dominance of those great social and cultural powers, those world forces which made the modern paradigm great and impelled it on with increasing speed, are now put in question: the unconditional and unbounded domination of

a science free of ethics;
an omnipotent macrotechnology;
an industry which destroys the environment;
a democracy which is purely a legal form.

The problems posed by the modern age to itself, which Theodor W. Adorno and Max Horkheimer already analysed immediately after the Second World War as 'the dialectic of Enlightenment',[55] have now largely become common property: it is in the nature of the rational enlightenment itself that its rationality easily turns into irrationality. Not all scientific progress is also human progress. An abyss still yawns between the hominized world and the world which has to be humanized. The limited particular rationality of science and technology is by no means entire, undivided rationality, truly rational rationality.

41

And a radical critique of reason, one which goes to the roots, necessarily attacks the roots of this reason and thus can easily destroy any rational legitimation of truth and justice. That is the reason why Adorno and Horkheimer see the Enlightenment caught up in an unstoppable process of self-destruction and call for an Enlightenment which transcends itself.

Let me say it once again: the evil produced by science and technology cannot simply be healed by even more science and technology. In particular, scientists and technologists stress today that while scientific and technological thought is capable of destroying a traditional ethic which has become alien to reality, much of the immorality which has been disseminated in the modern period is not the result of ill will but an unintended 'by-product' of industrialization, urbanization, secularization and organized irresponsibility. But modern scientific and technological thought has from the beginning proved incapable of providing the foundation for universal values, human rights and ethical criteria. In the meantime science has relativized itself - and this is to be regarded as a positive development - through Einstein's theory of relativity, Heisenberg's uncertainty principle and Gödels incompleteness theorem . . .

(b) Whence the binding ties?

It is a very welcome development that particularly since the 1980s, German philosophy, whether it derives more from linguistic analytical philosophy (Karl-Otto Apel[56]), from Frankfurt critical theory (Jürgen Habermas[57]), or from the theory of history (Rüdiger Bubner[58]) is again more concerned with praxis and thus with the rational foundation for a binding ethic. However, philosophy generally finds it difficult to provide the foundation for an ethic which is practicable for larger strata of the population and which is above all unconditional and generally binding.[59] Therefore a number of philosophers (from Alasdair MacIntyre[60] and Richard Rorty[61] to Michel Foucault[62] and Rüdiger Bubner[63]) prefer to dispense with universal norms and refer back to the customary features of a variety of worlds and forms of life. But do not all merely regional rationalities and plausibilities, precepts and laws, inevitably fall short, and must not fixations on regional and national interests constantly be broken off for the sake of the great whole?

However, the problem arises in particular for a 'discursive ethics'

42

(Apel, Habermas), which rightly stresses the significance of rational discourse and consensus, as to why we should prefer discourse and consensus to violent confrontation. And does discourse really imply morality and not just tactics? Should reason not provide a basis for the unconditioned nature and universality of its norms? But how can it do that once it can no longer refer back to a quasi-innate 'categorical imperative' (Kant)? It seems that previously philosophical justifications of unconditionally binding and universal norms hardly got beyond problematical generalizations and transcendental-pragmatic or utilitarian pragmatic models. Certainly (despite an overarching authority) they refer to an ideal community of communication, but they remain abstract and optional - and not just for the average person. Despite their claim to a transcendental 'ultimate binding quality' they do not seem to point to any universally obvious and unconditional obligation. Why should I do that unconditionally, and why should I in particular do it? Those who want to dispense with a transcendent principle have to follow a long path of horizontal communication with the possibility that in the end they have just been going round in a circle.

And as far as specific experience is concerned: philosophical models easily fail precisely at the point where an action is required of human beings in a specific instance - and this happens quite often - which is in no way to their advantage, which in no way serves their happiness or any communication, but rather can require of them an action against their interests, a 'sacrifice' which in an extreme case can even call for the sacrifice of their life. Philosophy quickly ends with the 'appeal to reason' where ethical obligation 'hurts' existentially. How can *that* be required of *me*? Indeed there is a question to which even Sigmund Freud, who appealed to reason for his ethics, had no answer: 'When I ask myself why I have always behaved honourably, ready to spare others and to be kind whenever possible, and why I did not give up doing so when I observed that in that way one harms oneself and becomes an anvil because other people are brutal and untrustworthy, then, it is true, I have no answer.'[64]

So can one face any danger of spiritual homelessness and moral arbitrariness with pure reason? Of course, since the sciences, technology and even philosophy are no help, many people go their own way. The interest of many of our contemporaries in horoscopes, which is incomprehensible to anyone with knowledge of astronomy, similarly

43

arises from this need for a basic orientation for important decisions in the future and for the widespread pressure for all kinds of more or less serious psychological 'aids to life'.

However, as we can see, the issue is not just one of private, personal decisions: the great economical and technological problems of our time have increasingly become political and moral problems (as has also been realized in the Club of Rome[65]), and these transcend and make excessive demands on any psychology, sociology and perhaps also philosophy. Who can tell us today, where we can do more than we dare, what we should do? Perhaps the religions, which are much praised and much disparaged? The religions, whose right to exist is fundamentally questioned by philosophy? The religions, which themselves have their intrinsic problems with theological ethics? We must discuss both these questions briefly.

2. The Recalcitrance of Religion

(a) A post-metaphysical age?

Some philosophers - often in conversation only with philosophers - intensely once again conjure up a 'post-metaphysical age' and 'post-metaphysical thinking' (J.Habermas)[66] in order to move forward from there to an ethic with a rational foundation. However, since they have grown up in a period and an intellectual milieu in which religion could still be identified with 'projection' or 'alienation' (Feuerbach), with social 'repression' or 'the opium of the people' (Marx), with 'regression' or psychological immaturity (Freud), and could be regarded as finished, they all too easily overlook the questionable empirical and epistemological presuppositions of their own 'post-metaphysical thought'. Certainly religion has been increasingly ignored, suppressed and finally (as in the French Revolution) persecuted in modern times, for understandable reasons - because it has been opposed to science, technology, industry and democracy (human rights!). But in the post-modern period the question once again arises: what future does religion have?

My standpoint here is that an analysis of our age which brackets out the religious dimension is deficient.[67] For like art or law - considered diachronically and synchronically - religion is a universal phenomenon: 'The fulfilments of the oldest, strongest and most urgent wishes of mankind' (Freud).[68] Its character as an 'illusion' has in no way been proved (even after Freud); its central content is, rather, a matter of a reasonable trust.[69] However, to neglect this universal human phenomenon in an analysis out of laziness, ignorance or resentment would be to fail to do justice to an essential dimension of human life and human history, whether one affirms it or denies it. Or is meaningless waiting for Godot to be preferred to a reasonable trust in God - understood as the all-embracing, all-penetrating last and first reality?[70]

(b) The end of religion?

If we look at East Germany, at Poland, at Czechoslovakia or the Soviet Union, at South Africa, Iran, the Philippines or Korea, and finally also at North and South America, today the cultural historical thesis of the end or the dying out of religion seems clearly to have been falsified. Neither atheistic humanism (à la Feuerbach) nor atheistic Socialism (à la Marx) nor atheistic science (à la Freud or Russell) has succeeded in replacing religion. On the contrary, the more the ideologies, these modern secular convictions of faith, lost credibility, the more the religions, old and new convictions of faith, gained impetus. Nowadays people talk of a postideological era but hardly still of a post-religious era.

At any rate, even in Western Europe, we cannot begin from a 'mass atheism' (in 1987 according to a Gallup Poll in the USA 94% believed in God; in 1989 according to an Allensbach Poll in West Germany 70% believed in God and 13% did not; at the beginning of 1990, according to the *Sunday Times* and *Sunday Telegraph*, in Great Britain three quarters of the population believed in a 'supernatural being'). Of course nowadays any Western religion is radically confronted with the problem of secularization. But secular worldly society does not in any way automatically mean religionlessness.

It is institutionalized religion, the Christian churches, which at least in Europe are in crisis because of fossilization and isolation (in the case of the Catholic church) or exhaustion and lack of profile (in the case of the Protestant church), which they have brought down on themselves. But given the present diffusion of religion and the zeal for conversion among fundamentalist or alternative communities there can be no question of a dying out of religion generally. The nihilism

45

prophesied by Nietzsche - whether as a matter of principle or of a practical, vulgar kind - is a fact, where belief in God has been lost. But to the degree that for many people belief in God is not dead, so too nihilism is not universal.[71]

In the past decades it has emerged more clearly than before that a religion can contribute not only to human oppression but also to human liberation: not only in psychological and psychotherapeutic terms, but also politically and socially. Here there is no longer propagation of a class morality (of a bourgeois stamp) of the kind that Marx and Engels rightly criticized in the last century;[72] here - from Latin America to Korea, from South Africa to the Philippines, from East Germany to Rumania - there is a struggle for a humane society. Here it has proved everywhere that religion can contribute in terms of social psychology to the furthering of freedom, to the observance of human rights and to the rise of democracy:

• Certainly religions can be authoritarian, tyrannical and reactionary and all too often were so in the past: they can produce anxiety, narrow-mindedness, intolerance, injustice, frustration and social isolation; they can legitimate and inspire immorality, social abuses and wars in a people or between peoples.

• But religions can also have liberating effects, orientated on the future and beneficial to human beings, and indeed often have had. They can disseminate trust in life, generosity, tolerance, solidarity, creativity and social commitment, and can encourage spiritual renewal, social reforms and world peace.[73]

And the most recent development of all has now demonstrated how beyond religions an ethic can be encouraged which previously has hardly been seen in this form: the virtually revolutionary power of an ethic of non-violence. For the first time in recent years, in autumn 1989 we experienced (in Leipzig and elsewhere) a revolution not with guns firing but with candles burning. However, this non-violent revolutionary movement was not headed either by conservative (and often devious) hierarchs of fossilized churches (the Catholic hierarchy in East Germany and the Orthodox of Rumania publicly rejected it) or by the many well-adapted 'grey church mice'. The points at which it crystallized were religious leaders (spiritual leaders, pastors or laity) who were dynamic and at the same time aware of their responsibilities, tolerant and open and at the same time consistently religious, and groups which developed a new style of leadership (like the team of the

46

Nikolai church in Leipzig or Pastor László Tökés in Rumania, who became the starting point of the revolution). Hence the question:

(c) Religion - a mere projection?

Epistemologically, the argument about projection in religious matters may be said to have been seen through: from a psychological perspective, belief in God (like any other faith, hope and love) naturally always displays the structure and content of a projection, and therefore is always under suspicion of being a projection. But the fact of projection by itself in no way decides whether the object to which my projection relates exists or not. Belief in God or a wish for God - which in themselves are not an argument either for or against God! - can correspond to a real God.[74] Of course it is still a fact that religion is claimed as a form of consolation governed by particular interests or an infantile illusion. But that need not be the case. Religion can also become the foundation of psychological identity, human maturity and a healthy self-awareness; indeed religion can, as I have indicated, become a decisive stimulant and the motive force for social change. And that is what it is today - to say this once again - more so than the philosophy which since Hegel at the height of modernity has been suffering far more than religion from a 'devaluation' (J.Habermas). Here I would expressly agree with Jürgen Habermas when he says: 'So I do not believe that we as Europeans can seriously understand concepts like morality and ethics, person and individuality, freedom and emancipation . . . without appropriating for ourselves the substance of a salvation-historical thought which originates in Judaism and Christianity.'[75]

But the question which Habermas does not answer is why I should now appropriate the 'substance' of the Jewish Christian tradition in a 'post-metaphysical context', a context of rational unbelief. Why not be a rational believer in a new way - since religion now is certainly not passé, but is alive psychologically and in a way which brings social liberation (a chief characteristic of postmodernity!)? Why should religion with its wealth of metaphor serve me as an expression of the overcoming of contingency and hope for redemption only so long as a post-metaphysical philosophy cannot offer me anything adequate here? Why should I not also give philosophical expression to the 'longing for the wholly Other' which cannot be stilled - unfortunately

Jürgen Habermas has never taken up this basic notion of his teacher Max Horkheimer? But - the counter question might perhaps now run - have not the religions for their part considerable problems internally in laying the foundation for an ethic?

3. Religious Difficulties with Ethics

(a) Fixed moral solutions from heaven?

Something has already long been clear to many religious people - above all Jews and Christians, but without doubt also, say, the adherents of Chinese religion - which some people nowadays in Islam and Hinduism also perhaps feel to be a problem. A first difficulty is that less than ever at the end of the twentieth century can we get fixed moral solutions from heaven or the Tao, or derive them from the Bible or any other holy book. That is not to say anything against the ethical commands of the Bible, the Qur'an, the Torah or Hindu and Buddhist scriptures with a transcendent foundation. But first of all it has to be conceded that from a historical perspective and according to all historical research the concrete ethical norms, values, insights and key concepts of the great religions have formed in a highly complicated social and dynamic process. It is easy to understand how where the needs of life, urgent human concerns and necessities emerged, there was also pressure for regulations for human conduct: priorities, conventions, laws, commandments, instructions and customs, in short, particular ethical norms. Therefore much that is proclaimed in the Bible as God's commandment is also already found in the ancient Babylonian Code of Hammurabi from the eighteenth and seventeenth centuries before Christ.

That means that human beings have had to test and still have to test ethical norms and ethical solutions in projections and models, often practising them and proving them over generations. After periods of proving and acclimatization, such norms finally come to be recognized, but sometimes - if the times have changed completely - they are also undermined and replaced. Are we perhaps living in such a time?

(b) Differentiated solutions on earth

Religious people, too, should also consider a second difficulty today; differentiated solutions have to be sought and worked out 'on earth' for all problems and conflicts. Whether as Jews, Christians, Muslims or as members of an Indian, Chinese or Japanese religion, people are themselves responsible for the concrete shaping of their morality. To what extent? To the degree that they too must begin from their experience, from the great variety of life, and must keep to the facts.

That means that even religious people cannot dispense with getting hold of confirmed information and knowledge about all the specific problem areas from bio- and sexual ethics to business ethics and state ethics, and operate everywhere with factual arguments, in order in this way to test what might help towards a decision and finally also to arrive at practicable solutions. Religious people in particular, who often have their heads in the clouds, must tell themselves nowadays that they may not appeal to so high an authority and deprive human beings of autonomy within the world. In this sense, what was worked out by Kant is true: there is an ethical legislation for ourselves and a responsibility for realizing ourselves and shaping our world which is innate to the conscience.

(c) Scientific methods

And religious people should note a third difficulty: given the reality of technological society which is so many-layered, changeable, complex and often impenetrable, the religions too cannot avoid making use of scientific methods in order to investigate as far as possible without prejudice the material laws and future possibilities of this society.

Certainly not every average Christian, Jew, Muslim, Hindu or Buddhist needs to make use of these scientific methods. Even today, of course, the pre-scientific awareness of particular ethical norms, in so far as it still exists, retains basic significance for a high proportion of believers. And happily many people still 'spontaneously' act correctly in particular situations without ever having read a tractate on moral philosophy or moral theology. Nevertheless, the wrong verdicts (for example in connection with war, race, the situation of women or the significance of birth control) which have found their way into many religions in the course of more recent history have shown that modern life has become too complex for it to be possible in defining specific ethical norms - particularly with regard to sexuality or aggression, and also economic or political power - in a naive blindness to reality to overlook empirical data and insights confirmed by science.

In positive terms, this means that nowadays a modern ethic is dependent on contact with the natural sciences and the human sciences: on contact with psychology and psychotherapy, with sociology and social criticism, with behavioural research, biology, cultural history and philosophical anthropology. The religions, their responsible leaders and teachers, should not show any anxiety in becoming involved in all these: the human sciences in particular offer them a growing wealth of relatively certain anthropological insights and information which is relevant to action, and these can be used to help in making decisions in a way that can be verified - even if they cannot replace the ultimate foundations and norms of human ethics.

In view of so many highly complex problems, however, every ethic continually finds itself confronted with explicit conflict situations and clashes of duty - in both the individual and the social spheres; seldom is a situation so clear that there are not also reasons for an opposite moral decision. What is one to do in that case?

(d) Rules for priority and certainty

Both for individuals (e.g. scientists) and for institutions (e.g. disciplines, research institutes and industries), in specific instances it is often very difficult to weigh up benefits (for example, in the individual sphere the life of the mother against the life of the unborn child; in the social sphere creation of work against danger to the environment). To facilitate the choice, which nowadays often displays quite different dimensions of space and time, present-day ethics has developed a whole series of rules for priority and certainty. I shall give a brief version of some of them here:[76]

1. A rule for solving problems. There must be no scientific or technological progress which, when realized, creates greater problems than solutions. An example is the elimination of a hereditary illness by human gene manipulation.

2. A rule for the burden of proof. Anyone who presents new scientific knowledge, approves a particular technological innovation, or sets going a particular form of industrial production, has to demonstrate that what is embarked on does not cause either social or ecological damage. Examples are the location of industries or the planting of genetically altered plants, bacteria and virus (as a means of combating blight) in the open air outside the laboratory.

3. A rule for the common good. Interest in the common good has

50

priority over individual interest - as long as (and this point has to be made against the Fascist 'common use comes before personal use') personal dignity and human rights are preserved. An example is stronger backing for preventive than for remedial medicine.

4. A rule of urgency. The more urgent value (the survival of a person or humankind) has priority over a value which is intrinsically higher (the self-fulfilment of a person or a particular group).

5. An ecological rule. The ecosystem, which may not be destroyed, has priority over the social system (survival is more important than better living).

6. A rule of reversibility. In technical developments reversible developments have priority over irreversible ones: there should be only so much irreversibility as is absolutely necessary. For example, operations involving gene surgery could alter all the genetic information system in a person, and germ-line engineering can have fateful effects on coming generations.

However, there is a problem. A rational ethic can recommend quite specific atittudes and lifestyles with particular rules - like limiting oneself, a capacity for peace, fair distribution, the furthering of life. However, the more specific one becomes, the more questions are raised about the moral motivation, the degree of compulsion, the general validity and the ultimate meaningfulness of norms generally. And it is precisely at this point that the religions have their own contribution to make.

4. The Religions - A Possible Foundation for Ethics

(a) Can what is humanly conditioned be an unconditional obligation?

Let us be quite clear: even those who have no religion can also lead a life which is authentically human and in this sense moral: this is the expression of human autonomy within the world.[77] But there is one thing that those who have no religion cannot do, even if in fact they want to accept unconditional moral norms for themselves: they cannot give a reason for the absoluteness and universality of ethical obligation. What remains uncertain is why I should follow such norms unconditionally, i.e. in every case and everywhere - even where they

51

run quite contrary to my own interest. And why should everyone do this? For what is an ethic worth in the last resort if it is not observed by everyone? What is an ethic worth in the last resort if it does not apply without any ifs and buts, unconditionally; not 'hypothetically' but 'categorically' (Kant)?

An unconditional claim, a 'categorical' ought, cannot be derived from the finite conditions of human existence, from human urgencies and needs. And even an independent abstract 'human nature' or 'idea of humanity' (as a legitimating authority) can hardly put an unconditional obligation on anyone for anything. Even a 'duty for humankind to survive' can hardly be demonstrated conclusively in a rational way. In the face of the apocalyptic potential of nuclear or genetic technology, Hans Jonas rightly raises a metaphysical question with which ethics has not previously been confronted: whether and why there should be a humankind the genetic heritage of which should be respected; indeed why there should be life at all.[78] It can probably be demonstrated on rational grounds that humankind as it has now in fact developed has no future, but on moral grounds is ripe for destruction (and who knows what Adolf Hitler might not have done at the end, had he had at his disposal not only the V2 but a superpower's present-day nuclear potential for destruction?). And as far as the appeal to individual reason in the specific case is concerned, 'human survival' is certainly not endangered by each individual *qua* individual (even if today, as is the case with not a few young couples, individuals practise a boycott on procreation) - so why should it be categorically required in the concrete instance?

Indeed - presupposing that no personal risk is involved - why should not a criminal kill his hostages, a dictator do violence to his people, an economic group not exploit its country, a nation not begin a war, a power bloc in an emergency launch rockets against the other half of humankind, if that is in their basic interest and there is no transcendent authority which holds unconditionally for all? Why should any of these unconditionally act otherwise? Is an 'appeal to reason' by means of which it is so often possible to justify one thing or its opposite enough?

(b) Only the unconditioned can be an unconditional obligation

Here I shall just state briefly the answer to be given in principle. Nowadays - after Nietzsche's glorification of 'beyond good and evil' -

52

we can no longer count on a 'categorical imperative' which is quasi-innate in all, and make the wellbeing of all human beings the criterion for our own action. No, the categorical quality of ethical demand, the unconditioned nature of the ought, cannot be grounded by human beings, who are conditioned in many ways, but only by that which is unconditional: by an Absolute which can provide an over-arching meaning and which embraces and permeates individual, human nature and indeed the whole of human society. That can only be the ultimate, supreme reality, which while it cannot be proved rationally, can be accepted in a rational trust - regardless of how it is named, understood and interpreted in the different religions.

At least for the prophetic religions - Judaism, Christianity and Islam - it is the one unconditional in all that is conditioned that can provide a basis for the absoluteness and universality of ethical demands, that primal ground, primal support, primal goal of human beings and the world that we call God. This primal ground, primal support and primal goal does not represent alien control over human beings. On the contrary: such grounding, anchorage and direction open up the possibility for true human selfhood and action; they make it possible to frame rules for oneself and to accept personal responsibility. So, properly understood, theonomy is not heteronomy, but the ground, the guarantee and also the limit of human autonomy, which may never deteriorate into human arbitrariness. Only the bond to an infinite offers freedom in the face of all that is finite. To this degree one can understand why after the inhumanities of the Nazi period, in the preamble to the Basic Law of the Federal Republic of Germany, the twofold dimension of responsibility (before whom and for whom?) has been retained: 'responsibility before God and humankind'.[79]

But whatever the basis for the unconditional character of the ethical demands in the various religions, whether these derive their demands more directly from a mysterious absolute or from a revealer figure, from an old tradition or a holy book, one thing is certain: religions can present their ethical demands with a quite different authority from a merely human one.

(c) The basic functions of religion

Religions speak with absolute authority, and they express this authority not only with words and concepts, teachings and dogmas, but also with symbols and prayers, rites and festivals - i.e. rationally and emotionally. For religions have means of shaping the whole of human existence, not just for an intellectual elite but also for broad strata of the population - means which have been tested by history, adapted to cultures and made specific for the individual. Religion certainly cannot do everything, but it can disclose a certain 'more' in human life and bestow it.

- Religion can communicate a specific depth-dimension, an all-embracing horizon of meaning, even in the face of suffering, injustice, guilt and meaninglessness, and also a last meaning of life even in the face of death: the whither and whence of our being.
- Religion can guarantee supreme values, unconditional norms, the deepest motivations and the highest ideals: the why and wherefore of our responsibility.
- Through common symbols, rituals, experiences and goals, religion can create a sense of feeling at home, a sense of trust, faith, certainty, strength for the self, security and hope: a spiritual community and allegiance.
- Religion can give grounds for protest and resistance against unjust conditions: the longing for the 'wholly Other' which is already now at work and which cannot be stilled.

True religion, which is related to the one absolute (God), is essentially different from any quasi- or pseudo-religion, which absolutizes and divinizes a relative, whether this is the atheistic 'goddess of reason' or the 'god of progress' with all its 'lesser gods' in the pantheon of modernity (which for a long time similarly have not been investigated): science (natural science), technology ('high tech') and industry ('capital'). Now in the postmodern period they all seem largely to have been demythologized and deideologized, in other words, relativized. And in this new world constellation we should not replace them with a new idol, for example the 'world market', to which all values would have to be subordinated, but with renewed faith in the one true God. True religion, which thus relates to the one and only absolute, again has a new opportunity in the postmodern period - no more and no less.[80]

But wherever one speaks of religion in this way or in any other, one will hear the objection that religions are by no means agreed among themselves, and that their statements are different, indeed contradictory, not only about the Absolute, but also about human ethics.

54

V. World Religions and a World Ethic

Indeed, have not the religions totally different and contradictory theoretical and practical concepts to offer? Are there not differences both in their doctrines and scriptures and in their rites and institutions, and finally also in their ethics and discipline? The members of the various religions usually know all too well where in practice they have spectacular differences from one another. For example, Christians know that Muslims and Buddhists have to abstain from alcohol in any form; the latter in turn usually know that alcohol is allowed to Christians. Jews and Christians know that Christians may eat pork, but Christians know that Jews and Muslims regard pork as unclean. Sikhs and strict orthodox Jews may not cut their beard or hair, but Hindus and also Christians and Muslims may do as they wish. Christians may kill animals, but Buddhists may not. Muslims may have several wives, but Christians may have only one. And so on.

But do the adherents of the various religions know equally well precisely what they have in common ethically? Not at all. So what unites all the great religions would have to be worked out carefully in detail on the basis of the sources - a significant and enjoyable task for the scholars of the different religions! But even at the present stage of the investigation some significant common views may be brought out briefly. It is not a matter of working out the differences and contradictions, the features of the great world religions which are exclusive and cannot be reconciled (I have discussed this in detail elsewhere[81]), but of working out what holds them together in spite of everything - with a view to the principle of responsibility. My question is: what can religions contribute to the furthering of an ethic, despite their very different systems of dogmas and symbols, that distinguishes them from philosophy, political pragmatism, international organizations and philanthropic concerns of all kinds? Here in brief I shall draw attention to six decisive perspectives.[82]

1. Ethical perspectives of the world religions

(a) Human wellbeing

Certainly, religions were and still are tempted to gather round themselves in order to preserve the power of their institutions, constitutions and hierarchies. And yet where they so wish, they can still credibly convey to the world, with a different moral power from that of many international organizations, that they are concerned with human wellbeing. For all the great religions authoritatively offer a basic religious orientation - support, help and hope in the face of the mechanism of all human institutions, in the face of the self-interest of the various individuals and groups, and in the face of the excess of information provided by the media.

To be specific, anyone in the prophetic tradition who truly believes in God should in practice consistently be concerned with human wellbeing. Hence the twofold Jewish commandment to love God and one's neighbour and its radicalization (to the point of loving one's enemy) in Jesus' Sermon on the Mount, along with the incessant demand of the Qur'an for justice, truth and good works. But the Buddhist doctrine of the overcoming of human suffering should also be mentioned here, along with the Hindu striving to fulfil 'dharma' and Confucius' requirement to preserve the cosmic order and thus the *humanum*. In all these instances human wellbeing and dignity as the basic principle and goal of human ethics is brought out with unconditional authority - in a way in which only the religions can and may do it. That means human life, integrity, freedom and solidarity in quite specific instances. Human dignity, human freedom and human rights can thus not only be stated in positivistic terms, but also be given a basis in an ultimate depth, a religious basis.

(b) Maxims of basic humanity

Certainly religions were and always are tempted to fix themselves on and encapsulate themselves in special traditions, mysterious dogmas and ritual precepts. And yet where they wish, they can establish the validity of fundamental maxims of basic humanity with quite a different authority and power of conviction from that of politicians, lawyers and philosophers. For all the great religions in fact call for particular 'non-negotiable standards', basic ethical norms and maxims for guiding action, which are grounded in an Unconditioned, an Absolute, and therefore are also to hold unconditionally for hundreds of millions of people.

To be specific, five basic commands to human beings which also have countless applications in the business world and in politics, hold in *all* the great world religions: 1. Do not kill; 2. Do not lie; 3. Do not steal; 4. Do not practise immorality; 5. Respect parents and love children. To many people these commandments may sound general. But how much would have to change and should change if, say, people again became generally aware of the commandment 'Thou shalt not steal' and it were applied to the evil of corruption (which unfortunately is increasingly rife even in states which were formerly intact in this respect)?

Such norms, when regarded as unconditional, are protection against an unprincipled libertinism which lives only for the moment and is exclusively concerned with the situation. Conversely, however, such norms should not be applied in the spirit of an un-free legalism which wants to keep to the letter of the law, quite undisturbed by the specific situation. In complex questions like birth control, termination of pregnancy or euthanasia, one cannot simply turn up the solutions in the Bible or in any other sacred book.

Here it must always be remembered that ethics is neither dogma nor tactics. Neither the law (legalistic ethics) nor the situation (situation ethics) should dominate by themselves. For norms without the situation are empty, and the situation without a norm is blind. Rather, norms should illuminate the situation, and the situation should govern the norms. Certainly what is moral is not just what is good or right in the abstract but what is good or right in the specific instance: what is appropriate. In other words, obligation becomes specific only in the particular situation. But in a particular situation, which of course can be identified only by the person involved, the obligation can become unconditional. That means that our 'ought' is always related to the situation, but in a particular situation the 'ought' can become categorical, without ifs and buts. So in any concrete moral decision the universal normative constant is to be bound up with the particular variables which are conditioned by the situation.[83]

(c) A reasonable middle way

Certainly, religions were and still are tempted legalistically to harp on some rigorist extreme positions, in both individual and social ethics, in both sexual and business and state ethics. And yet where they want to, they can win over hundreds of millions of people on this earth for a reasonable middle way between libertinism and legalism. For all the great religions in fact encourage models for action which indicate a middle way - so important given the complexity of individual and collective biases, emotions and interests.

To be specific, there is a middle way between greed and contempt for possessions, hedonism and asceticism, sensuality and hostility to the senses, succumbing to the world and denying it. We might think of the cultic and social duties which structure the whole life of a Hindu; Buddhist 'composure' in dealings with the world or the teaching of Confucius aimed at wisdom; the commandments of the Torah and Talmud which indicate to people their duties in the world before God; the preaching of Jesus, which is neither legalistic nor ascetical; or the many reasonable instructions of the Qur'an which are orientated on everyday demands: in all these instances, what is required is action which is conscious of a responsibility - towards oneself and the environment. All religions require not only the observance of certain rules, but particular dispositions, attitudes, 'virtues', which can guide human conduct from within, all the things that legal precepts cannot achieve in precisely the same way. Translated into the present social situation, the reasonable middle way would mean a way between ignorant rationalism and lachrymose irrationalism, between credulity towards science and condemnation of it, between euphoria at technology and hostility to it, between mere formal democracy and totalitarian democracy of the people.

(d) The golden rule

Certainly, religions were and still are tempted to lose themselves in an endless tangle of commandments and precepts, canons and paragraphs. And yet where they so will, they can explain with quite a different authority from that of any philosophy why the application of their norms does not apply from case to case, but categorically. Religions can provide a supreme norm for conscience, that categorical imperative which is immensely important for today's society, an imperative which obligates in quite a different depth and fundamental way. For all the great religions require observance of something like

58

a 'golden rule' - a norm which is not just hypothetical and conditioned but is categorical, apodeictic and unconditioned - utterly practicable in the face of the extremely complex situation in which the individual or groups must often act.

This 'golden rule' is already attested by Confucius: 'What you yourself do not want, do not do to another person' (Confucius, c. 551-489 BCE);[84] it is also in Judaism: 'Do not do to others what you would not want them to do to you' (Rabbi Hillel, 60 BCE to 10 CE),[85] and finally in Christianity: 'Whatever you want people to do to you, do also to them.'[86] Kant's categorical imperative could be understood as a modernization, rationalization and secularization of this golden rule: 'Act in such a way that the maxims of your will at any time can be taken at the same time as the principle of a universal legislation,'[87] or, 'Act in such a way that you always use humankind, both in your person and in the person of anyone else . . . at the same time as an end, never as a means.'[88]

(e) Moral motivations

Certainly, religions were and still are tempted to command people in an authoritarian way, to call for blind obedience and to violate the conscience. And yet where they so will they can offer convincing moral motivations. For in the face of so much frustration, lethargy and apathy, especially in today's younger generation, they can offer convincing motives for action on the basis of age-old tradition in a contemporary form: not only eternal ideas, abstract principles and general norms, like philosophy, but also the living embodiment of a new attitude to life and a new lifestyle.

To be specific: up to the present day motivation has been provided by those models for life which are depicted in the life and teaching of the great leading figures of the world religions: in the Buddha, in Jesus Christ, in Con-futse or Lao-tse, in the prophet Muhammad. Knowledge of the good, its norms, models and signs, are now communicated to the individual socially. And here it makes a quite decisive difference to someone whether a new lifestyle is lectured about beforehand in the abstract or whether an invitation can be given to it with reference to a compelling, specific model for such a lifestyle: to follow Buddha, Jesus Christ, Con-futse, Lao-tse or the prophet Muhammad.

(f) A horizon of meaning and identification of a goal

Certainly, religions were and still are tempted to have a double morality, namely to preach ethical demands only to others and not first apply them self-critically to themselves. But if they so will, even today - or again today - in the face of emptiness and meaninglessness for hundreds of millions of people they can credibly demonstrate with a unique power of conviction a horizon of meaning on this earth - and also a final goal.

To be specific: all religions offer an answer to the question of the meaning of everything, of life, of history, in the light of an ultimate reality which already has an effect here and now - whether this is described with classical Judaism as 'resurrection', with Christianity as 'eternal life', with Islam as 'paradise', with Hinduism as 'moksha', with Buddhism as 'nirvana' or with Taoism as 'immortality'. Precisely in the face of many frustrations and many experiences of suffering and failure, religions can help to lead people on by offering meaning beyond death and giving meaning here and now, not least where moral action has remained unsuccessful.

2. The special commitment of world religions

(a) Criteria for evaluation and distinction

A common world ethic therefore needs not only the great universal coalition of believers and non-believers; also and in particular it needs the special commitment of the different religions. What would it mean if all the representatives of the great religions ceased to stir up wars, and began to encourage reconciliation and peace between the peoples? What would it mean if the demands for social justice and the preservation of creation were no longer neglected but supported with full moral power? What would all this mean for hundreds of millions of people on this earth?

Without the support of the great religions, which can address individuals in their consciences ('hearts'), for example the duty of voluntary limitation which to which Hans Jonas rightly admonished people in his speech on receiving the Peace Prize in the Pauluskirche in Frankfurt in 1987, the 'duty to restrain our power, to curtail our enjoyment, for the sake of a future humanity' [89] can hardly be put into practice on a broad basis. Nor can demands like those of the Zurich social ethicist Arthur Rich: 'We must return from an economy of more and more to an economy of enough.'[90] The Frankfurt social ethicist Friedhelm Hengsbach has demonstrated in an illuminating way that it was the great movements with social and ethical motivations, often passed over by representatives of business and economics (the workers' movement, the women's movement, the environmental and peace movements) which in our century brought about an ethical transformation of industrial capitalism.[91] But who would be better suited today than the world religions to mobilize millions of people for a world ethic? To mobilize them by formulating ethical aims, presenting key moral ideas and motivating them both rationally and emotionally, so that the ethical norms can also be lived out in practice?

Conditions - from gene technology to the international debt crisis - are too complex for it simply to be possible directly to deduce scientific, economic, medical or social solutions and even concrete indications for action from any ethical principles and norms. But for the wellbeing of humankind ethical principles and norms can and should be introduced into the discussion and into concrete decisions: a framework of criteria with a rational or religious foundation for a common fundamental world ethic which can also serve to provide a basis for human rights and make them more profound and more specific.

(b) Global vices and virtues?

What I already addressed in the introduction to this book needs to be repeated here: only a beginning can be made here on the complex questions of an ethic which would bring the world religions together.[92] Specialists are invited to make further advances. In the process it may presumably also have to be demonstrated that there are also parallels in all the other religions to the Christian catalogue of virtues and vices: thus for example the seven principal or root sins, as they have been listed since Gregory the Great: pride, envy, anger, covetousness, lust, gluttony and sloth (religious and moral); or also to the four cardinal virtues taken over from the Greeks, of wisdom, justice, courage and moderation. According to the ethics of the world religions are there not something like universal sins, something like 'world vices', and happily also virtues which are called for universally, something like 'world virtues'? If this is the case, why should not the world religions find themselves in the fight against world vices and the encouragement of world virtues?

It would certainly be easy to confirm this in the light of the other religions. For example, when in Buddhism contentment and lack of envy are highly valued; when the world is to be esteemed and not simply to be exploited; when human beings are always to be regarded as an end and never as a means; when knowledge means more than riches and wisdom more than knowledge; when mourning is no reason for despair: then one will probably be able to find parallels to these attitudes - for all the difference in the overall context. Or when the Muslim attaches particular importance to a sense of order and a striving for justice, when the virtues of courage and composure are given a particularly important place, and at the same time the Muslim is to be distinguished by consideration, humility and a spirit of community; here one can certainly find parallels for all these virtues in Judaism and in Christianity.

(c) A first common declaration

Granted, what I have sketched out here is of course an ideal programme: religions *could* do this if they wanted to. That reality often mocks such a programme in all the great world religions is, of course, well-known. In all the world religions (as in most states), there is a failure to realize human rights; there are tensions and indeed conflicts between the specifically religious ethic and a general humane ethic. For example in Catholic Christianity there is the prohibition against artificial contraception; in Islamic fundamentalism the treatment of women, dissidents and non-Muslims; in Hinduism the maintaining of the caste system, and so on. All these are serious questions for the religions, but do not in themselves refute the high ethical demands in these religions themselves. However, the religions become credible only when they begin by radically applying to themselves the ethical criteria which they themselves propagate, wherever they preach them to 'the world'.

Conversely, however, it is also unmistakable that a growth of awareness of their global ethical responsibility has begun in the religions themselves. Here it has emerged that what ultimately matters in ethics is not the various theoretical systems of reference but what should be done or not done quite practically, in life as it is lived. And in connection with this praxis, people from the various religions who are religious in the best sense of the word have constantly kept finding and understanding one another. Whether particular tormented, violated or rejected people are ultimately helped on the basis of a Christian or Buddhist, Jewish or Hindu attitude may initially be all the same to those concerned. And to this degree, in matters both small and great, it is possible to arrive at a common view of what to do and not to do, even if the theoretical presuppositions and implications of the various religions are completely different.

This is impressively confirmed by a declaration which was made by the 'World Conference of the Religions for Peace' as early as 1970 in Kyoto, Japan. It expresses in an admirable way what could be a concrete universal basic ethic, a world ethic of the world religions in the service of world society:

'Bahai, Buddhist, Confucian, Christian, Hindu, Jain, Jew, Muslim, Shintoist, Sikh, Zoroastrian and others - we have come together in peace out of a common concern for peace.

As we sat down together facing the overriding issues of peace we discovered that the things which unite us are more important than the things which divide us. We found that we share:

- A conviction of the fundamental unity of the human family, of the equality and dignity of all human beings;
- A sense of the sacredness of the individual person and his conscience;
- A sense of the value of the human community;
- A recognition that might is not right, that human power is not self-sufficient and absolute;
- A belief that love, compassion, unselfishness and the force of inner truthfulness and of the spirit have ultimately greater power than hate, enmity and self-interest;
- A sense of obligation to stand on the side of the poor and the oppressed as against the rich and the oppressors;
- A profound hope that good will finally prevail.'[93]

These statements are good, but some will object that they are still far too general. And without doubt, they can be made concrete. Therefore to end this first part, on a world ethic, I shall ask: Has perhaps Christianity - more ravaged than other religions by the movement of secularization but also more challenged by it - already made a more specific contribution to a possible world ethic? The answer to that is: certainly so far Christians have not had such a world ethic directly in view, but certain Christian declarations can be used in this direction.

VI. Specific Christian Contributions

The Christian churches met in October 1988 in Stuttgart on a German level, in May 1989 in Basle on a European level and finally in March 1990 in Seoul on a world level. In all cases the programmatic concern was the furtherance of 'Justice, Peace and the Integrity of Creation'. The Basle document in particular,[94] which unfortunately was not followed by any document at an equivalent level in Seoul because of the disparity between the statements of delegates, is a model Christian contribution for the postmodern period.

1. A Model Christian Contribution

(a) Self-criticism by the church

In contrast to the approach of some documents of the Vatican and the World Council of Churches, the Basle assembly did not just preach to the world in a self-righteous way, but first exercised self-criticism on the church. The Christian churches have become aware of their own failings in the past. Here is the wording of their convincing self-criticism:[95]

- We have failed, because we have not borne witness to God's caring love for each and every creature and because we have not developed a lifestyle which corresponds to our understanding of ourselves as part of God's creation.
- We have failed, because we have not overcome the divisions between the churches and because we have often used the authority and power given us to strengthen false and limited solidarities like racism, sexism and nationalism.
- We have failed, because we have caused wars and not exhausted all the possibilities of devoting ourselves to mediation and reconciliation. We have excused wars and often too easily justified them.
- We have failed, because we have not questioned decisively enough the political and economic systems which misuse power and riches, which exploit the natural resources of the world only for their own

use and perpetuate poverty and marginalization.

- We have failed, beause we have regarded Europe as the centre of the world and have thought ourselves superior to the other parts of the world.
- We have failed, because we have not constantly borne witness to the sanctity and dignity of all life and the respect that we owe all men and women equally, and also the need to give all people the possibility of exercising their rights . . .

But authentic Christianity (like some other religions) is not content with a confession of guilt, but calls for radical change as a consequence, the change which politicians, social planners and psychologists, parties and associations find it so difficult to achieve: a change in awareness, in psychological attitude, in the whole mentality, at the centre of a person, in the 'heart'. Indeed Christianity aims at a change in human beings from the centre - of men and women in their confrontation with the Unconditioned, the Absolute, God himself. This is what is meant by the biblical word *meta-noia*; a basic 're-thinking', a 'con-version' of men and women, of humankind, to the Absolute, to God.

(b) A new basic consensus on integrative human convictions

No one nowadays need any longer be opposed to 'modern achieve-ments', to freedom, equality and brotherhood, to democracy and human rights, because he or she believes in God. Nowadays a religious orientation to reality and a scientific view of the world are no more mutually exclusive than religious faith and political involvement. Two hundred years after the French Revolution, happily not only most states but also most Christian churches have in principle affirmed the basic values and basic convictions of the French Revolution, which they had rejected for so long and which unfortunately they have yet to realize within Catholicism (in respect of women, priests and theo-logians). But we may say - and this thought was current in the Anglo-Saxon rather than the French Enlightenment - that Christian faith can provide an even more convincing basis for what can hardly be grounded in purely empirical terms; the special relationship of human beings to God ('the image of God') can radically provide a basis for that which transcends all empiricism:

- the autonomy of the human person;
- the inalienable freedom of the human being;

66

- the equality of all men and women in principle;
- the necessary solidarity of all men and women with one another.

However, 200 years after the French Revolution the affirmation of the modern convictions of 'freedom, equality and brotherhood' - which are often misunderstood in individualistic terms and practised in a one-sided way - are no longer enough. In the postmodern period they in particular need the dialectical counterpoint, the supplementation and 'sublation' which I would like to attempt here, quoting, developing and accentuating the theses of the 1989 European assembly in Basle:[96]

2. Postmodern Requirements

(a) Not just freedom, but also justice

For the next millennium a way must be found to a society in which men and women possess equal rights and live in solidarity with one another:

a way from the differences between poor and rich, between powerful and powerless, which divide us;

a way from the structures which cause hunger, deprivation and death;

a way from the unemployment of millions of people;

a way from a world in which human rights are violated and men and women are tortured and isolated;

a way from a way of life in which moral and ethical values are undermined, if not rejected altogether.

What we need is a social world order!

(b) Not just equality, but also plurality

For the next millennium a way must be found to a reconciled multiplicity of cultures, traditions and peoples in Europe:

a way from divisions which form boundaries and which are furthered by racial, ethic and cultural discrimination;

a way from contempt for and marginalization of two-thirds of the world;

a way from the legacy of antisemitism in our societies and churches and its tragic consequences.

What we need is a pluralistic world order!

(c) Not just brotherhood, but also sisterhood

For the next millennium a way must be found to a renewed community of men and women in church and society in which women bear an equal share of responsibility to men at all levels and in which they can freely contribute their gifts, insights, values and experiences:

- a way from divisions between men and women in church and society;
- a way from the devaluation and lack of understanding of the indispensable contribution of women;
- a way from the ideologically fixed roles and stereotypes of men and women;
- a way from a refusal to acknowledge the gifts given to women for the life and decision-making processes of the church.

What we need is a world order in partnership!

(d) Not just coexistence, but peace

For the next millennium a way must be found to a society in which peacemaking and the peaceful resolution of conflicts is supported, and to a community of peoples which contribute in solidarity to the well-being of others:

- a way from wars and ideologies, which scorn the divine in every human being;
- a way from the idolatry both of the concrete structures of power and of militarism;
- a way from the destructive consequences of the giant sums now being spent on armaments;
- a way from a situation in which military intervention or the threat of military intervention seems necessary to preserve or implement human rights.

What we need is a world order which furthers peace!

(e) Not just productivity, but solidarity with the environment

For the next millennium a way must be found to a community of human beings with all creatures, in which their rights and integrity are also respected:

- a way from a separation between human beings and the rest of creation;
- a way from human domination over nature;

a way from a lifestyle and economic means of production which severely damage nature;

a way from an individualism which violates the integrity of creation in favour of private interests.

What we need is a world order which is friendly to nature!

(f) Not just toleration, but ecumenism

For the next millennium a way must be found to a society which is conscious that it needs constant forgiveness and renewal, and which together thanks and praises God for his love and for his gifts:

a way from the divisions in which the churches still live;

a way from the mistrust and the enmity in their dealings with one another;

a way from the burden of paralysing memories of the past;

a way from the intolerance and the refusal to acknowledge religious freedom.

What we need is an ecumenical world order!

It is probable that consciousness of our global responsibility for the future of humankind has never been so great as it is now. Abstinence in matters of ethics is no longer possible.

It has become abundantly clear why we need a global ethic. For there can be no survival without a world ethic.

B. No World Peace without Religious Peace

An ecumenical way between fanaticism for truth and forgetfulness of truth

I.   The Two Faces of Religion

Perhaps I may be allowed to begin this second part with a personal reminiscence. Around a quarter of a century ago - to be more precise, in April 1967 - the centenary was being celebrated of what was then the most significant academic institution in the Near East, the American University in Beirut. Muslim and Christian theologians were invited to give festival lectures: from the Christian side Dr Visser't Hooft, the then General Secretary of the World Council of Churches; Cardinal Johannes Willebrands, later President of the Vatican Secretariat for Unity; and myself, as a theological Benjamin. Beirut, the city at the point of intersection between Christianity and Islam: what an opportunity for the encounter of religions, what a unique opportunity to experience Muslim theologians directly as conversation partners! However, things turned out differently.

1. Religions at War

(a) The case of Lebanon

A remarkable thing happened: Muslim theologians were nowhere to be seen when we appeared, and none of us Christian theologians had a chance to meet them. Why not? Because in accordance with the programme they had all already spoken a week before us. When I personally asked Charles Malik, the President of the Congress, at that time Lebanese Foreign Minister and President of the United Nations General Assembly, why now - after the Second Vatican Council with its pioneering declarations on religious freedom and the attitude of the church to Judaism and Islam - Christian and Muslim theologians had not been invited together, his answer was: 'Cher Professeur, c'est trop tôt!' 'It's too early!' In 1967 - too early!

At that time Lebanon was still regarded as the 'Switzerland of the Near East', a peaceful island in the midst of regions and religions which were being fiercely fought over. But already at that time whispers could be heard in Lebanon that the situation was explosive, that the political balance between Christians and Muslims was fluid, that the Christian predominance was endangered by the growth in the Muslim population, and that the present constitution could not be maintained in the long term. However, would things turn out so badly for this rich-poor land? No one could really suspect so at the time.

I have not forgotten this Beirut experience. Now - after one of the longest and most fearful civil wars in history - I can put it in context. For I have come to the conclusion - and Lebanese have endorsed this insight - that had a serious religious dialogue between Christians and Muslims in Lebanon been sought twenty-five years ago, and had this been supported by the religious communities, Lebanon would not have slithered into a catastrophe of this dimension. A religious understanding could have served as a basis for a reasonable and just political solution. A fanaticism of violence, murder and destruction fed by the religions could thus have been mitigated. In the spirit of a Christian renunciation of power, already in the early 1970s Christians would voluntarily have been able to make those concessions to the Muslims which were subsequently wrung from the Gemayel government by force of arms in the 1980s and which then could no longer pacify the land. In short, the civil war and immeasurable bloodshed could have been avoided. Instead of gruesome chaos, Lebanon would now have stood as a model of ecumenical understanding. And I am convinced - I shall put this in a single sentence: Like Lebanon, so too the state of Israel and the city of Jerusalem can find peace and continued existence only through religious and political dialogue between Jews and Muslims, Israelis and Palestinians, and not through a sixth, seventh and eighth war. Is all that an illusion?

(b) Negative consequences

Of course the question may rightly be asked: can religions contribute so much? There is no disputing that in negative, destructive terms they have made and still make an enormous contribution. So much struggle, bloody conflicts, indeed 'religious wars' are to be held to their account; so many economic, political and military conflicts have been partly started, partly coloured, inspired and legitimated by religions - and this also goes for the two world wars.

Many massacres and wars not only in the Near East between Maronite Christians, Sunni and Shi'ite Muslims, between Syrians,

Palestinians, Druse and Israelis, but also between Iran and Iraq, between Indians and Pakistanis, Hindus and Sikhs, Singhalese Buddhists and Tamil Hindus, and earlier also between Buddhist monks and the Catholic regime in Vietnam, as also today between Catholics and Protestants in Northern Ireland, were or are so indescribably fanatical, bloody and inexorable because they have a religious foundation. And what is the logic? If God himself is 'with us', with our religion, confession, nation, our party, then anything is allowed against the other party, which in that case must logically be of the devil. In that case even unrestrained violation, burning, destruction and murder is permissible in the name of God.

However, there are examples to the contrary.

2. Religions at Peace

(a) Germany, France, Poland as opposite examples

Religions can also contribute an infinite amount in a positive sense, towards building up, and have done so. They can intervene through individuals, religious groups or whole religious communities in a tenacious way for peace, social justice, non-violence and love of neighbour in the world. They can propagate and activate basic attitudes like readiness for peace, renunciation of power and tolerance. Here are just two political examples.

1. For centuries France and Germany were regarded as archenemies. In the nineteenth and twentieth centuries they waged three great wars in a nationalistic spirit, two of which developed into world wars. The world owes the fact that after the Second World War the old resentment did not revive and a politics of revenge no longer dominated to men like Charles de Gaulle, Konrad Adenauer, Maurice Schuman, Jean Monnet and Alcide de Gasperi. As great politicians they did not think primarily in bureaucratic and technocratic terms along Brussels lines, but because of their fearful experiences they pursued (quite realistically in political terms) a vision with an ethical and religious foundation. That put an end, once and for all, to these wars between European nations. A united Europe on a Western, Christian foundation, bound together economically and politically in defence is the best guarantee that in future the nations will live

together in peace. And to make it clear that the reconciliation of France and Germany after so much anti-Christian devilry came from a Christian spirit, de Gaulle and Adenauer sealed this reconciliation before the world at the cathedral in Rheims, where the French kings were crowned.

2. After the Second World War the ideological fronts between the Federal Republic of Germany and the states of the Warsaw Pact were fully hardened. How - after the unprecedented atrocities of Germans in the East and the expulsion of millions of Germans from their ancestral homes - could there be mutual forgiveness? Already at the end of the 1950s Julius Döpfner, then Bishop of Berlin and later Cardinal of Munich, took a first step towards reconciliation with a bold appeal. But he was quickly silenced by a storm of indignation. It was the Evangelical Church in Germany which ventured a new attempt in 1965. Through a theologically well-argued and politically balanced memorandum it prepared for reconciliation beween Germans on the one hand and Poles, Czechs and Russians on the other. This made possible years later not least that policy of treaties with the East which, even if one might criticize it in details, in fact proved to be a tolerable basis for a provisional political normalization until the great revolution finally came in 1989.

(b) No world peace without religious peace

Examples can be multiplied: I could have mentioned the Civil Rights Movement in the United States in the 1960s, which was started by a black pastor, Martin Luther King, and was supported by many pastors, priests and nuns. I could have mentioned the peace movement of the 1980s and 1990s, which is headed by people with religious motivations - above all Christians and Buddhists - from the USA to Japan, from Northern Ireland and Eastern Europe to South Africa. I could continue, but instead of this I shall ask, with a view to the future:

What would it mean for tomorrow's world if the religious leaders of all religions, great and indeed small, decided today to give resolute expression to their responsibility for peace, love of neighbour and non-violence, for reconciliation and forgiveness? If from Washington to Moscow, from Jerusalem to Mecca, from Belfast to Teheran, from Amritsar to Kuala Lumpur, instead of helping to foment conflicts they were to help in resolving them? All the religions of the world today

75

have to recognize their share in responsibility for world peace. And therefore one cannot repeat often enough the thesis for which I have found growing acceptance all over the world: there can be no peace among the nations without peace among the religions. In short, there can be no world peace without religious peace.

Constructive engagement with the other religions of this world for the sake of peace in the world is vitally important for survival. In the third millennium - following the example of Europe - we shall have either a quite different peaceful 'ecumene' or we shall have no 'ecumene', no 'inhabited earth' at all. In 1988 computer photographs were published of the part of the Milky Way most remote from our cosmos (4C41.17); it is fifteen billion light years away from us. No, in view of the immense size of the universe and our own boundless human overestimation of ourselves, a God of creation and evolution is truly not dependent on our little planet, which flies along on the periphery of galaxies which go into hundreds of millions. Conversely, this planet is desperately in need of a God of creation and evolution. This insight compels us to perceive our responsibility for one another and to abandon our dogged stubbornness in dealings with one another. And this applies centrally to what is perhaps the most disputed question in religion, the question of truth.

II. The Question of Truth

Happily, on the tiny spaceship earth there is increasing awareness, from Roman Catholicism to Far Eastern Buddhism, of a responsibility for world peace and religious peace. How much did it already mean that in 1987 in Assisi, before the eyes of the whole world, the Pope and the Dalai Lama, representatives of Judaism, Christianity and Islam, along with representatives of Indian and Far Eastern religions, prayed for world peace in a way which could be seen, even though they were separated?

1. The Task

(a) Awareness is at different stages

And yet there was just as sharp criticism of the Assisi meeting as there was of the granting of the Leopold Lukas prize (founded for understanding among the nations by the son of a Jewish scholar who was gassed in a concentration camp) to the Dalai Lama by the Protestant theological faculty of the University of Tübingen - an expression of a terrifying disparity of stages of awareness in the most different strata of the churches and religions. Remarkable coalitions of interest are suddenly forming out of groups which otherwise have little in common: Catholic traditionalists around Archbishop Lefebvre arm in arm with fundamentalist Protestants, both of whom conjure up the spectre of syncretism and the diffusion of faith, both of whom fear the betrayal of Christian mission and set themselves up as self-nominated defenders of the one truth, the 'Christian' truth. Such disparities - the product of different historical paradigms - must be taken seriously, and the difficulties in overcoming the problems should not be trivialized. For it has to be conceded that there can be no peace among the religions without a clarification of the question of truth.

(b) Between fanaticism for truth and forgetfulness of truth

Clarification seems unavoidable, because no question in the history of the churches and religions has been the cause of the shedding of so

77

much blood and tears as the question of the truth. Blind fanaticism for the truth has at all times and in all churches and religions brought unbridled violation and murder. Conversely, forgetfulness of the truth, lack of orientation and loss of norms have meant that many people no longer believe in anything.

In view of this situation the basic question in inter-religious understanding and the peace movement is: is there a theologically responsible way which allows Christians and those of other faiths to accept the truth of other religions without giving up the truth of their own religion and thus their own identity? There are three strategies which can be adopted towards the question of truth, but it seems to me that none of them can make any contribution to a resolution of the question of peace which has political relevance.[97]

2. Three Strategies - No Solution

(a) The fortress strategy

With more or less confidence and self-righteosness it is presupposed that:

- Only one's own religion is the true religion. All other religions are untrue.
- Religious 'peace' is guaranteed only through the one true (state) religion.

For a long time that was the official Roman Catholic position (*Extra Ecclesiam nulla salus* - Outside the church there is no salvation!). As if the church were already the kingdom of God! As if God's Spirit were not also at work in all other religions, which indeed are all provisional!

In fact this narrow-minded standpoint of exclusiveness or superiority, accompanied by phobias about contacts, can also be found in other churches: in Protestant fundamentalism in the USA, and often also in German pietism; sometimes also in other religions, for example in Islam. Everywhere there is the same spirit of intolerance, absolutism of truth and self-righteousness which has caused so much misery to people. Associated with this religious imperialism and triumphalism is a self-opinionated theological apologetic which is incapable of learning and causes more problems than it solves.

Already in the 1960s the Second Vatican Council achieved a bold move, from ignoring, despising and condemning other religons to tolerating them, respecting them and recognizing their significance for salvation. After affirming dialogue in principle and carrying on inter-religious consultations, in the 1990s the World Council of Churches has still to make this decisive move to outward-directed ecumenism. Ecumenism between the Christian confessions must be followed by real, if different, ecumenism between the great religions. No, a fortress strategy is no solution.

(b) The strategy of playing down differences

Widespread above all among enlightened Western people, this follows the following slogans:
- The existential problem of 'truth' does not really exist since each religion is equally true in its own way, in its essence.
- Religious 'peace' will best be achieved by ignoring the differences and contradictions.

And indeed, does not what is allegedly the same religious, 'mystical' experience underlie all religions? The answer to this is 'no', since every religious experience is *a priori* interpreted; it is an experience shaped and structured by a particular religious tradition. And anyone who really knows the religions which are at present competing with one another can hardly claim that they are all similar and thus also equally true. A discernment of the spirits (true-untrue, good-evil) cannot therefore be made from there. This would level out not only the fundamental differences between the basic types of mystical, pro-phetic and wisdom religion but also all the contradictions between the individual religions themselves. It would amount to a failure to recog-nize that even an individual religion has not simply remained the same in the course of its history, but has developed and become complex - to an often amazing degree. Are all religions equally true? This thoughtless strategy of playing down differences does not really do justice to any religion; a religious pot-pourri is not the solution. And just as everything is not simply one, so too everything is not simply the same - even in one's own religion. 'Anything goes' can least of all silence the basic questions of human life about truth and meaning, about values and standards, about what is ultimately binding and can be relied on. Or precisely in the religious sphere is everything already to be legitimate because it happens now ('the power of the factical') and possibly comes along in picturesque garb (religion in the guise of folklore)?

So there is a need to avoid not only exclusivist mediaeval Roman or Protestant fundamentalist absolutism but also that enlightened modern relativism which plays down differences, which makes all truths, values and criteria a matter of indifference and precisely in so doing passes over the reality of human life. A modern optional pluralism which is current today among intellectuals, which indiscriminately approves one's own and the other religions, a theological indifferentism for which all religious positions and negations are equally valid and thus a matter of indifference, and which spares itself the trouble of 'discerning the spirits', is not a real solution. In view of the only too real and often fatal rivalry between religions, it ignores the problems that it claims to have solved. No, a strategy which plays down the differences is not a solution either.

(c) The strategy of embrace

This conception is beyond question more subtle and is advocated by both Christians and non-Christians:

- Only one religion is the true one, but all religions which have grown up in history have a part in the truth of this one religion.
- Religious 'peace' will best be achieved by the integration of the others.

Is this the most convincing strategy? It seems to be. For if a standpoint of exclusivism which recognizes no truth outside its own is as unacceptable as a relativism which 'relativizes' all truth and without distinction approves and confirms its own and the other religions, would not then the standpoint of a generous, tolerant inclusivism be the best solution?

We encounter this strategy - if we leave aside the speculative and unrealistic theory of Christian theologians which sees non-Christians (Jews and Muslims) as supposedly 'anonymous Christians'[98] - above all in religions of Indian origin.[99] All empirical religions represent just different levels, stages, partial aspects of the universal truth of one's own religion. The other religions, including those of Semitic and prophetic origin, are not regarded as untrue, but as provisional. They

80

are said to have a share in the one universal truth (Hindu, Buddhist or even Taoist). So a 'higher (deeper) knowledge' can be claimed for one's own religion with an appeal to mystical experience.

What is the consequence? Any other religion is in fact deposed to a lower or partial knowledge of the truth. One's own religion is given a place as a preliminary stage or partial truth but it is denied a special claim of its own. So what looks like toleration in practice proves to be a kind of conquest through embrace, a matter of allowing validity through domestication, an integration through a loss of identity. No serious religion which seeks to remain true to itself will allow this to happen to it. This strategy, too, is not a real solution to the problem of truth and thus a real contribution to peace among the religions and nations. No, a strategy of embrace is no solution. But what could help? What would be the truly ecumenical strategy? Before we come to that, however, we must consider something else.

3. Self-criticism: The Presupposition for an Ecumenical Strategy

(a) Not everything is equally good and true

So with what basic attitude should the adherents of the religions deal with the question of truth, in a way that would be significant for world peace? The unconditional presupposition for a truly ecumenical strategy seems to me to be self-criticism by every religion, a critical look at one's own history of failure and guilt. For any unprejudiced person knows that the boundary between truth and untruth is not *a priori* identical with the boundary between one's own religion and any others. Those who keep their heads will concede that the boundaries between truth and untruth often run through one's own religion. How often we are right and wrong at the same time!

A criticism of the other position can therefore be justified only on the basis of resolute self-criticism. In principle: in the religions, too, not everything is equally true and good; there is also that which is not true or good in doctrines of faith and morality, in religious rites and customs, institutions and authorities. And why should not each religion have a mirror held up to it here by the other religions, which have their own experiences?

Of course this is also true of Christianity. And if people today rightly

81

condemn the aggressiveness of particular representatives of Islam who refer to the threat in the Qur'an of death for those who deviate from the faith, as a Christian one should not forget that Christianity has a terrible history of the persecution of heretics and those of other beliefs (above all the Jews). Since the emperor Theodosius the Great, who in 391 declared Christianity the state religion and banned other cults, heresy has been regarded as a crime against the state. So the enemy of the church is also the enemy of the empire and is punished accordingly. As early as 385 the Spanish heretic Priscillian was executed for heresy in Trier along with six companions in Trier. Martin of Tours and others had objected. Ambrose, Pope Siricius and Christianity in general condemned what seems to have been the first killing of Christians by other Christians for differences in belief. But people got used to it. Pope Leo the Great already pronounced himself satisfied with these proceedings. Not to mention the later fury of the Inquisition: in Seville alone in 1481 around 400 people were burned; by the year 1783 the number of those burned is given as 31,000. And who does not know that the connection between the Inquisition and witch-hunting in Catholic and Protestant areas led to actions which make one's hair stand on end, and was only dismantled at a relatively late stage...

(b) The critical mirror of the world religions

Christians who have never been challenged by adherents of other religions are far too little aware of how sharp the criticism of Christianity from the world religions is.[100] It is said that Christianity,

despite its ethic of love and peace is often exclusive, intolerant and aggressive in its manner and activity: in short, it is loveless and unpeaceful;

exaggerates almost pathologically the consciousness of sin and guilt in human beings who are said to be corrupt at heart, so that it can then stress all the more emphatically the necessity of their redemption and their need for grace;

on top of everything falsifies by its christology the figure of Jesus, who is almost always seen in positive terms in the other religions, so that he is made an exclusive divine figure.

Is it a historical coincidence, people ask, that after centuries of highly intensive missionary work in Asia, where two thirds of humankind lives, Christianity has been able to win over only around five per cent of the population?

Whatever the justification of this criticism may be, it shows that the question of truth and falsehood cannot be dismissed in a religion, in any religion. Think of all that is taught and practised in the name of the religions. There is no innocent religion. All religions have their pluses, and they also have their minuses. Or is perhaps everything allowed in the name of religion?

(c) Is everything allowed in the name of religion?

For that reason the basic question has to be raised here - not just in connection with, say, Islam and Teheran, but also in connection with Christianity and Rome: can all means be hallowed by religious ends? Is everything allowed in the service of religious devotion - including the misuse of economic and political power, human sexuality or aggressiveness?

To put the question in a more pointed way: may what appears inhuman, what manifestly damages, violates, perhaps even destroys people, be a religious commandment? There is a wealth of examples in any religion. Are human sacrifices to be justified because they are offered to a god? On grounds of faith may children be sacrificed, women burned, heretics be tortured to death? Does prostitution become worship because it takes place in a temple or is engaged in for inspiration? Are perhaps both praying and cursing, asceticism and sexual promiscuity, fasting and the use of drugs, marital fidelity and adultery to be justified in the same way if they serve as means and ways to 'mystical experience'? If one is against termination of pregnancy may one also be against artificial contraception? Are even charlatanism and fraudulent miracles, every possible form of lying and deception, allowed, because this happens for an allegedly 'sacred' end? Is magic which seeks to compel the deity the same as religion which prays to the deity? Are imperialism, racism or male chauvinism, are hatred of witches, Jews or Turks, to be affirmed where they appear with a religious foundation? May a price be put on peoples' heads because they are allegedly heretics or apostates? Are there even no objections to a mass suicide, as in Guyana, as long as it has a religious motivation? I think that the answer is no, in all cases no!

But in that case from where do we derive the criteria for what is true and false, good and evil, in the different religions?

III. The Quest for Ecumenical Criteria for Truth

We can easily see how tricky and difficult the question of criteria for truth is if these criteria derive only from subjective whim or are simply to be foisted on the other religions. Here we have to note the legitimate difference in perspectives. Self-criticism can come about in any religion in two ways: not just through perceiving and welcoming criticism from outside, but also through measuring it by one's origins.

1. Measuring by Origins

(a) Normative writings or figures

The sharpest criticism of any form of untruth in religions is immanent in the religions themselves. How often have the religions become unfaithful to their own 'nature', their own origins? For:

- Normative for all religions are their holy books: the Bible, the Qur'an, the Bhagavadgita, the Discourses of the Buddha, the Chinese classics . . .
- Normative for almost all religions are holy figures: the Christ, the Prophet, the Wise Man, the Buddha . . .

Indeed, how often have the religions had to be reminded by their critics and reformers, prophets and wise men, that they were in a bad state, that they had become untrue to their nature? In other words: this distinctive original 'nature' which is peculiar to every religion, its normative 'origin' or 'canon' ('standard'), is in different ways a valid internal criterion of truth for each religion, which at the same time guarantees its own identity. 'Why do you come to disturb us?' This question put by the church's Grand Inquisitor to the Christ who returns in Dostoievsky's book has already made many Christians aware of its own authentic critics (Greek *krisis* = separation, distinction, decision, judgment).

84

(b) The need for one's own specific criteria for truth and their limitation

No religion will be able completely to avoid also applying its own quite specific criteria of truth to the other religions, whether these are Christian, Jewish, Islamic, Hindu, Buddhist or Confucian. Dialogue does not mean self-denial. And criticism from outside remains necessary. But anyone who remains sober and honest knows that these criteria can primarily be relevant to, and indeed binding on, one's own religion only, not others.

So if any religion were simply to insist on its own criteria for truth in dialogue, there would be no prospect of any genuine dialogue from the start. Take, for example, the Bible. Certainly, as the original testimony to Christ the New Testament has a decisive critical and liberating function in discussions between the Christian churches, as does the Hebrew Bible in discussions between Christians and Jews. But already in conversation with Muslims, who regard the Bible as a holy book (but one which has been falsified by Jews and Christians), and even more with Hindus and Buddhists, a direct appeal to the Bible as a criterion for truth would be inappropriate. Or would Christians allow themselves to be convinced if the question of truth were decided in the light of the Qur'an, the Bhagavadgita or the Discourses of Buddha? But - and here is the difficult question - what is left if in the dialogue between religions, Jews and Christians may no longer simply refer to the Bible (or Muslims to the Qur'an, the Hindus to the Gita or the Buddhists to their canon) as an indisputable authority, so that they can be in the right, in the truth, over against others?

2. A Fourth, Ecumenical Strategy

(a) Universal ethical criteria

With all due caution, here I shall attempt another way, sketch out a fourth strategy. I hope that it will contribute both to peace among religions and to the preservation and testing of their truth.

If we compare our religions with the others, but also if we reflect on the misuse of our own religion, then in the case of every religion the question will arise as to universal criteria of truth and goodness, which

85

are applicable in an analogous way to all religions. This, it seems to me, is important not least for questions of law and peace between the nations.

In addition to specific criteria which, as we saw, each religion has for itself, today more than ever we need to discuss universal ethical criteria. Here there is no mistaking that religion has always proved most convincing where it has succeeded - long before any modern attempts at autonomy - in effectively establishing what is truly human, the *humanum*, against the horizon of the Absolute: one need only mention the Decalogue ('the Ten Commandments'), the Sermon on the Mount, the Qur'an, some Discourses of the Buddha and the Bhagavadgita. Any religious message today, including the Christian message, has, however, to be rethought against the new horizon of a changed world.

(b) The late realization of human rights in Christianity

In modern times, Christianity above all other religions has had to undergo a painful process of change, but this is now also extremely significant for the other religions. As is well known, within the Christian sphere of influence, during the modern process of Enlightenment and emancipation a humanism (often secularist and hostile to the church) has emerged as a critic of religion, appealing to reason, nature and conscience. For a long time, therefore, Christianity has resolutely opposed such autonomous humanistic ideals as freedom of faith, conscience and religion.

It has been wrong to do so. Why? Not just because Christianity has ultimately profited from this process of autonomy, but because freedom, equality, brotherhood and 'human dignity' (the embodiment of the *humanum* in codified law, as is evident for example from Article 1 of the Basic Law of the Federal Republic of Germany) were originally Christian values which had been 'rediscovered' here and realized with strict consistency for modern times. The authors of the American Declaration of Human Rights were not atheists, but enlightened (deistic) believers in God. And some revolutionaries felt that the Human Rights of the French Revolution of 1789 should have originally been passed 'in the name of God', though this did not prove possible. But Rome in particular and the Roman Catholic church (and in part also other churches) condemned human rights as un-Christian - until the change of course under John XXIII and the Second Vatican Council after the middle of our century.

However, once the *humanum* had emancipated itself from religion and the church in modern autonomy, it could finally once again find a home in the sphere of Christianity - above all other religions - though the full realization of human rights (in respect of women, theologians and dissidents) has still to be achieved in the Roman system itself (the Vatican, the last absolutist monarchy in Europe, has not only to sign the declaration of human rights of the Council of Europe but still has *glasnost* and *perestroika* before it).

(c) The religious foundation for human values

Secular society, too, must be concerned that the *humanum* should retain a place within a religion, specifically in our case within Christianity. For a consideration arises here to which I drew urgent attention in Part A: precisely at a time of loss of orientation and the disappearance of ties, a time of 'widespread permissiveness and shameless cynicism', Christianity and indeed religions generally - beyond any psychology, educational theory, legislation and politics - can again play a decisive role for the individual conscience, giving it backing, emotional support, security, consolation and courage to protest. In the fight for the *humanum*, religion can unambiguously provide reasons that politics cannot: as to why morality and ethics should be more than a matter of personal taste or political opportunism, a question of individual judgment, social convention or communication. In other words, religion can unambiguously demonstrate why morality, ethical values and norms must be unconditionally binding (and not just where it is convenient for me) and thus universal (for all strata, classes and races). Precisely in this way the *humanum* is rescued by being seen to be grounded in the *divinum*. It has proved that only the Unconditioned can itself impose an unconditional obligation, and only the Absolute can be absolutely binding.

(d) Progress in the direction of humanity

There is also no mistaking the fact that for the 'cultured despisers of religion' (to use Schleiermacher's phrase), in the question of the *humanum*, since modern times a process of reflection has begun in all

87

religions, progress in the direction of humanity - despite all the failure and despite all the time-lags in awareness. We have to think of:

- The abolition of the inquisitorial practices with fire and torture customary in Roman Catholicism until well into modern times, and the humanization of Catholic canon law (though in many respects it is still inhumane);
- The abolition of human sacrifices and suttee in India, practices which were rejected from the beginning by Indian Buddhists and Christians but continued in isolated areas of India until the English occupation;
- A more humane reinterpretation of the doctrine of the *jihad* ('holy war') in Islam; the reforms of penal law in progressive Islamic countries; criticism within Islam of the *shariah,* that mediaeval sacral law which is sometimes in striking contradiction to the 1948 United Nations Universal Declaration of Human Rights, in particular in respect of equal rights for women (in marriage, divorce, inheritance and work) and for non-Muslims (for example in prohibited professions).

Numerous conversations in the Far East, Middle East and Near East have convinced me that in the future a marked increase in awareness might be observed in all the great religions in respect of the following central human concerns:

- The preservation of human rights;
- The emancipation of women;
- The realization of social justice;
- The immorality of war.

None of these are sheer utopias. Why should humankind, which in its long history has abolished particular customs like incest, cannibalism and slavery, not also be able to abandon, say, wars, in a completely new constellation in world history? Wars are certainly in no way part of human nature, like aggression and sexuality; they are not innate but learned, and can be replaced by a peaceful regulation of conflicts which does not resort to war. In the atomic age wars between atomic powers are suicidal, and wars between small countries with great allies usually remain undecided.[101]

IV. The *Humanum* as a Basic Ecumenical Criterion

So the hope that I expressed in connection with the call for a world ethic is not unjustified, that where a framework of ethical criteria is concerned, despite all the difficulties, in time an elementary basic consensus about the basic premises of human life and society within a world community could emerge at the level of a modern, humane awareness: what W.Korff calls 'leading convictions',[102] in other words basic human values and demands which could even be given a legal codification (as 'human rights' or 'basic rights').

1. Human Dignity as a Basis

(a) A first colloquium on religion at UNESCO

The seriousness with which the question is now viewed even at a global political level is shown by a colloquium which took place in Paris between 8 and 10 February 1989 and for which I was able to provide the basic report. The involvement of the educational organization of the United Nations in matters of world religion was a new development, but quite consistent. People have recently been realizing in this organization that changes in the direction of more 'brotherhood' (and 'sisterhood') among the nations, of more implementation of human rights and responsibility for peace, cannot succeed against the religions but only with them. There are religions in the countries of Africa and Asia, the Near East and Middle East, which still have quite a different kind of direct influence from that of religion in post-Enlightenment Europe. In his address at the opening of the colloquium the Director General of UNESCO, Federico Mayor, also stressed the significance of the world religions for the UNESCO programme 'Education in Human Rights'. The perception of the difference between the religions certainly does not exclude the quest for unitary values. Indeed the international community cannot exist without common values.

Unity in distinction - this programmatic phrase of UNESCO - presupposes an awareness of such things held in common. So from that angle, too, the question of a common basic criterion is pressing.

(b) What is truly human as a universal criterion

Should it not be possible to formulate, with reference to the common humanity of all men and women, a universally ethical, truly ecumenical basic criterion which is based on the *humanum*, that which is truly human, and specifically on human dignity and the basic values which are subordinate to it? The basic ethical question in terms of criteria is: What is good for human beings? The answer is: What helps them to be what is not at all obvious, i.e. truly human.

Accordingly, the basic criterion is: human beings should not be inhuman, purely subject to their drives, 'bestial', but should live in a rationally human, a truly human way. So that would be morally good which allows human life to succeed and prosper in the long term in its individual and social dimension: what enables the best possible development of men and women at all levels (including the levels of drives and feelings) and in all their dimensions (including their relationship to society and to nature).

2. The Relationship between Religion and Humanity

(a) Religions between humanity and inhumanity

Should it not be possible for all religions to agree at least on this basic question of criteria: what is good for human beings is what helps them truly to be human? According to this basic norm of authentic humanity, it is possible to distinguish between good and evil, true and false. So it is also possible to distinguish between what is basically good and bad, true and false, in an individual religion. One can formulate this criterion positively or - often more effectively - negatively in respect of religion:

- Put positively: a religion is true and good to the degree that it serves humanity, to the degree that in its doctrine of faith and morals, its rites and institutions, it advances men and women in their identity, sense of meaning and sense of dignity, and allows them to attain to a meaningful and fruitful existence.

90

- Put negatively: a religion is false and bad to the degree that it disseminates inhumanity, to the degree that in its doctrine of faith and morals, its rites and institutions, it hinders men and women in their identity, sense of meaning and sense of dignity, and thus does not allow them to attain to a meaningful and fruitful existence.

We can also put it another way: what is human, truly human, what has human dignity, can with justification appeal to the 'divine'. But what is inhuman, 'animal', 'bestial', cannot with justification appeal to the 'divine'. However, here a question arises: according to this theory does not the *humanum* take on as it were the function of judge on the religions, though they are grounded in the divine?

(b) Religion and humanity: a dialectical relationship

Indeed, with the *humanum*, is not a kind of 'superstructure' built over the concrete religions by which the religions are now to be judged and even condemned? Is not the *humanum* - the result of European humanism influenced by Christianity - a typically Western criterion, which does not apply at all to the Eastern religions? Is the *humanum* not from the start too vague as an ecumenically common criterion to be binding on the religions? And is not such a basic structure caught in a vicious circle? That is not the case, but there is - as has to be granted - a dialectical reciprocal understanding. It can be defined in the following way:

- True humanity is the presupposition for true religion. That means that the *humanum* (respect for human dignity and basic values) is a minimal requirement of any religion: where authentic religious feeling is to be realized, there must at least be humanity (that is a minimal criterion). But in that case why religion?
- True religion is the fulfilment of true humanity. That means that religion (as the expression of all-embracing meaning, supreme values, unconditional obligation) is an optimal presupposition for the realization of the *humanum*: there must be religion, in particular (that is a maximal criterion) where humanity is to be realized and made concrete as a truly unconditioned and universal obligation.

(c) A possible consensus

It was exciting to see that in the course of the Paris conference[103] a consensus began to emerge between the representatives of the various

91

religions:[104]

- No representative of the religions accepted an 'autonomous *humanum*' as a superstructure over the concrete religions. All affirmed for their religions that the *humanum* must be rooted in the Absolute (in an ultimate and supreme Reality, understood in whatever religious way).
- All representatives accepted self-criticism as a presupposition for inter-religious dialogue. All conceded that in the name of their religions human dignity and human rights were still being violated, violence and hatred were often being stirred up, peace frustrated and destruction inflicted.
- All agreed that particularly in the religions, action was needed to train men and women for humanity and a capacity for peace. No one contradicted the programmatic statement of the whole symposium: 'No world peace without religious peace.'
- All the representatives of the great world religions affirmed in principle the possibility of grounding humanity in their own traditions. Humanity could thus become the basis of a common ethic of the world religions.

So humanity was not regarded as an 'invention' of the West. Quite the opposite.[105] From the Jewish side one could hear that 'Judaism undoubtedly has a classical religious basis for affirming a universal ethical reality.' The Muslim spoke of the Qur'an as the 'ideal codex of human rights' and referred to a very recent official Muslim declaration on human rights of 1988. The representative of Hinduism spoke of a close connection between morality and religious feeling and of the need for resistance against the self-destructive forces in the world. Even the Buddhist said that the recognition of the trans-anthropocentric and cosmological dimension of human beings in Buddhism did not exclude their specific human significance in the universe or make it impossible. Precisely the wisdom of Buddhism with its strong stress on 'compassion' implied 'the recognition and affirmation of each and all in their difference and in their uniqueness'. The Confucian went furthest, being able to stress from the great humanistic tradition of Confucianism: 'The quest for ecumenical criteria poses no problem for the Confucian tradition. The *humanum* has always been the central concern of Confucianism.' All this might support the considerations that I put forward in the first part of my plea for a world ethic.

However, there is another question. Is not the identity of the individual religion lost in a dialogue of religions, in so much forming of a consensus? Does not the capacity for dialogue basically mean the absence of a standpoint?

V. Capacity for Dialogue and Steadfastness are not Opposites

Indeed, does not the truth become relative by virtue of sheer plurality? One can feel for oneself that here a fundamental question is pressing for an answer. And particularly those who are engaged in inter-religious dialogue have to put this question to themselves sooner or later. Is capacity for dialogue a demand of the time? Can it not be used as an excuse for conveniently not adopting a standpoint? For the surrender of firm convictions, for the squandering at rock-bottom prices of ties that have grown up? Is capacity for dialogue by itself already enough to give credibility? Is it already enough to want to carry on dialogue 'about everything' and 'with everyone', without any obligation, without a standpoint, indeed without practising steadfastness in dialogue oneself? Does not the very capacity to engage in dialogue presuppose that I and my partner have a standpoint about which it is worth engaging in dialogue? So might it be possible that someone who had given up everything was not really capable of dialogue? Is dialogue solely for those who are still prepared to hold fast to the truth of their own standpoint? The semantic field of the word 'steadfastness' can already teach us something.[106]

1. What is 'Steadfastness'?

(a) A neglected virtue

What is meant by 'steadfastness'? Certainly not a moralizing 'rigidity', a 'stubbornness' of the 'thus and in no other way' kind; certainly no rigid holding on to outdated positions, no love of self which indulges in favourite habits. What is it, then? A look at current theological or etymological dictionaries will be disappointing: there are satisfying explanations of dialogue and capacity for dialogue, but there is nothing (or only a few lines) on 'steadfastness'. Even the more recent psychological, educational and sociological lexicons evidently find it unnecessary to waste thought on this term. In this connection the 'U-turns' of a politician, the temperamental nature of a chef, the 'softness' of a judge are not seen as virtues. Rather, particularly in politics and public life, the requirement, wish, demand is to stand firm, to stand up, to stand fast: this is firmness as opposed to U-turns or going soft, 'steadfastness' quite generally as a basic attitude, a virtue, and therefore the ability to be steadfast in a particular situation in the face of temptations or pressures.

(b) Constancy and resistance

In steadfastness one can recognize an old, classical virtue as compared with capacity for dialogue. In the classical doctrine of virtues it was first to be put alongside the cardinal virtue of bravery.[107] Even more closely related to modern steadfastness is constancy, *constantia*, the classical virtue of the ancient Romans, though this is mentioned only once in the Latin New Testament - in Acts 4.13, where it renders the *parrhesia*, the 'boldness' of Peter and John. *Con-stare* means stand fast, maintain a firm attitude, remain stable, steadfast, true to oneself, consistent. *Constantia* means a firm attitude, direction, stability, steadfastness and therefore also constancy, persistence, consistency, stamina, intrepidity, courage.[108]

So steadfastness in this context is connected with resistance to external powers and those in power; with self-assertion, not giving in, holding firm; with courage, resolution, executive ability - all this with the freedom and responsibility of the individual in view. So precisely in the light of the classical tradition steadfastness is not a rigid and static reality, but a dynamic reality which proves itself in the processes of life. There was a reason why for the ancients bravery was always connected with cheerfulness, generosity and openness. For Christians, all this is grounded in faith in God and in the one whom God himself raised from death to life, who as the weak and helpless one was himself appointed 'Kyrios' and 'Christos' by God. But does not precisely such a standpoint of faith *a priori* rule out a dialogue with believers of other convictions?

2. Invitation to Dialogue

(a) Is a standpoint of faith a block to dialogue?

Does not precisely such steadfastness in faith represent a block to serious dialogue between religions? Or to put the question in even more concrete terms: if one believes in Christ as the way, the truth and the life, can one then also accept that there are other ways, other truths, that there is other life from transcendence? The Torah? The Qur'an? The Eightfold Path of the Buddha? So can openness and truth, plurality and identity, capacity for dialogue and steadfastness, be combined in inter-religious dialogue? That is the main question in any inter-religious undertaking. Is there a theologically responsible way which allows Christians to accept the truth of other religions without giving up the truth of their own religion and thus their own identity?

Slogans like 'indifferentism', 'relativism' and 'syncretism' are always being hurled against inter-confessional and inter-religious dialogue. Let me make it quite clear: I too repudiate indifferentism, relativism and syncretism which do not display any clear standpoint. But a pure negation is not yet a critical position. It is important to differentiate here.

(b) A critically ecumenical standpoint

If we are to combine steadfastness and readiness for dialogue, we will first be able to describe an ecumenical position like this. What we have to strive for is:
- No indifferentism for which everything is of equal value, but more indifference over alleged orthodoxy which makes itself the criterion for human salvation or damnation and seeks to impose its claim to truth by means of power and compulsion;
- No relativism for which there is no Absolute, but rather more sense of relativity in all that human beings make absolute and that prevents a productive co-existence of the various religions, and of relationality, which makes it possible to see every religion in its web of relationships;
- No syncretism, where everything possible and impossible is mixed together and fused, but more will for synthesis, for slow growing

together in the face of all confessional and religious oppositions and antagonisms which still cost blood and tears every day, so that peace can prevail between the religions instead of war and strife.

(c) Truth in freedom

In view of all the intolerance with a religious motivation, toleration and religious freedom cannot be called for enough. There can be no betrayal of freedom for the sake of the truth. But the reverse also applies: there can be no betrayal of truth for the sake of freedom. The question of truth may be neither trivialized nor sacrificed for the utopia of a future world unity and a single world religion. Particularly in the Third World, where the history of colonization and the history of mission mixed up with it are still by no means forgotten, this is rightly regarded as a threat to cultural and religious identity.

My understanding is that as Christians we are challenged to reflect again on the question of truth in the spirit of freedom with a Christian foundation. For in contrast to arbitrariness, freedom is not simply freedom *from* all ties and obligations, in a purely negative sense, but at the same time, positively, as I explained in Part A, freedom *for* new responsibility: towards fellow men and women, those around us and the environment, and the Absolute. So true freedom is a freedom for the truth.

Self-critically, all this means that the Christian, too, has no monopoly of the truth, but does not have the right to dispense with the confession of truth in the form of a random pluralism either. Dialogue and testimony do not exclude each other. Confession of the truth includes the courage to recognize untruth and to say what it is.

3. What are the Criteria between Religions?

(a) Three different criteria

From the need to distinguish between true (good) and false (bad) religion in all religions there follows the urgent necessity of a system of inter-religious criteria for all religions, which I can now sum up as follows:

● According to the general ethical criterion a religion is true and good if and insofar as it is human, does not suppress and destroy humanity, but protects and furthers it.

- According to the general religious criterion a religion is true and good if and insofar as it remains true to its own origin or canon, to its authentic 'nature', its normative scripture or figure, and constantly refers to it.
- According to the specifically Christian criterion a religion is true and good if and insofar as it shows the spirit of Jesus Christ in its theory and praxis.

Directly, the specifically Christian criterion can only be applied to Christianity: on the basis of the self-critical question whether and to what extent the Christian religion is Christian at all. Indirectly - and without any arrogance - the same criterion can certainly also be applied to the other religions: to the critical illumination of the question whether and to what degree in other religions, too (particularly in related Judaism and Islam), there is something of that spirit which we describe as Christian.

By analogy to the specifically Christian criterion there are also, as I have explained, specifically Jewish, Islamic, Buddhist, and other criteria, which we need not go into further here. Instead, the Christian criterion brought into play here must be protected from misunderstanding.

(b) The specifically Christian criterion

What is nowadays proclaimed as a 'brand new' doctrine[109] sometimes simply proves to be old doctrine from the spirit of Protestant liberalism, which certainly 'also' really heard God speak through Jesus and his message, but abandoned the normativeness and 'finality' of Jesus Christ - indeed had reduced him to the level of a prophet 'along with others' and so had lost all the criteria for discerning the spirits. Karl Barth and 'dialectical theology' (including Rudolf Bultmann and Paul Tillich) had rightly protested against such liberalism. A step back from that is hardly progress.

So those who as Christian (!) theologians are not prepared to give up this normativeness and finality of Jesus Christ do not adopt this position primarily because the other religions could only 'adapt to our modern technological world' with Christ as a critical catalyst, but because to do otherwise would be to abandon the central statement of all the scriptures which are normative for them, and which almost two thousand years ago came to form the New Testament, the foundation document of Christianity. Whether it is convenient or not, Jesus is normative and definitive for the whole of the New Testament: he alone is the Christ of God (the oldest and briefest confession of faith in the New Testament: *Iesous Kyrios*),[110] he is 'the way, the truth and the life'.[111] By contrast, for the Jews the Torah, for the Muslims the Qur'an, for the Buddhists the Eightfold Path, is 'the way, the truth and the life'.

If as a Christian one holds fast to the two-thousand-year-old conviction of Christianity - without anxiety or apologetic interests, but for good reasons, just as in the end Jews, Muslims, Hindus and Buddhists also hold fast to theirs - one is in no way involved in a theological 'imperialism' and 'neocolonialism' which denies truth to the other religions and repudiates other prophets, enlightened figures and wise men. Here - if we are to avoid the basic defect of both absolutist-exclusivist and relativist-inclusivist positions - a distinction must be made between the view of religions from outside and the view from within (however one might name this). Only in this way is a differentiated answer to the question of the truth of religions possible.

(c) Outside and inside perspectives

Seen from outside, as it were considered in terms of the study of religions, there are of course different true religions: religions which for all their ambivalence at least in principle correspond to particular general criteria (both ethical and religious). There are different ways of salvation (with different saving figures) towards the one goal, which can even partly overlap and which at all events can mutually fructify one another.

Seen from inside, i.e. from the standpoint of believing Christians orientated on the New Testament, and thus for me, as someone who is affected and challenged, there is only one true religion: Christianity, insofar as it bears witness to the one true God as he has made himself known in Jesus Christ. However, the one true religion in no way excludes truth in other religions, but can allow their validity: with qualifications they are true religions (in this sense 'conditioned' or in some way 'true'). In so far as they do not directly contradict the

Christian message, other religions can supplement and correct Christian religion and make it more profound.

Is that perhaps a contradiction? No, this interweaving of outside and inside perspectives can also be found in other, non-religious spheres. Here is just one example from the political sphere from which we began in this Part B. In negotiations even the statesman (the diplomat) and in lectures even the constitutional lawyer must begin from the fact that the other state in principle has its own equally legitimate constitution; that its law is equally obligatory and binding for its citizens. However, this view can and should be completely consistent with a person's intrinsic basic attitude. As a loyal citizen of the state among other citizens he or she feel themselves obligated in knowledge and conscience to this particular constitution (and no other); they see themselves as owing a uniquely binding loyalty to this state and this government (and to no other). I think that the best negotiator may be the one who can ideally combine both perspectives: the best possible loyalty to his or her own land (constitution, confession or religion) and a maximal openness to others.

That makes it clear that a maximal theological openness to the other religions in no way calls for the suspension of one's own convictions in faith. As if one could require of those who participate in religious dialogue that first of all they should give up their conviction of faith! Particularly in the interest of a global ethic to be supported by all religions from their own tradition, the question has to be asked:

4. What Does Readiness for Dialogue without Steadfastness Lead To?

(a) The consequences of a free-floating dialogue

Indeed, what would be the consequences of a dialogue without any normative rooting in one's own tradition? Put in the form of theses, the answer can only be: those who renounce the normativeness of their own tradition and begin from the equivalence of the various 'Christs' (Moses, Jesus, Muhammad, Buddha, Krishna, Confucius),

- already presuppose as a result what would not necessarily be desirable even at the end of a long process of understanding: such a method seems aprioristic;
- put the various leading figures paratactically alongside one another,

100

as if they were not partly dependent historically (for example Jesus on Moses and Muhammad on Jesus) and each had a completely different status within a religion (just as there are differences between the position of Moses in Judaism, of Jesus in Christianity, of Muhammad in Islam, of Krishna in Hinduism, of Buddha in Buddhism). Such a perspective seems unhistorical;

- expect of their non-Christian partners in dialogue what most of these reject: that they should give up *a priori* their belief in the normativeness of their own message and their bringer of salvation and adopt the standpoint that in principle all ways are equally valid (which is typically Western, secular and modern). Such a way seems unrealistic; it would be literally unworldly to call on a Buddhist to give up the normativenes of the Buddha (his way and his teaching), a Jew to give up the normativeness of the Torah, or a Muslim to give up that of the Qur'an;

- expect Christians themselves to demote the Christ Jesus to a provisional messiah and abandon the conviction of faith in the normative and definitive word of God given with Jesus Christ and called for by the New Testament, in favour of an identification of Jesus Christ with other bearers of revelation and bringers of salvation (putting 'Kyrios Iesous' on the same level as 'Kyrios Kaisar' or 'Kyrios Gautama'). From the perspective of the New Testament such a standpoint should be regarded as non-Christian - though of course there should be no witch-hunting of those who hold it.[112]

(b) And in practice?

In practice, all this means that those who adopt such a standpoint, whether as Christians or non-Christians, run the risk of parting company with their own faith-communities (whether voluntarily or involuntarily), and indeed giving up essential elements of their own religion. It is not much use to the dialogue between the religions if some Western (and Far Eastern) intellectuals come to some 'inter-religious' agreement. Indeed, it now becomes quite clear that basically no dialogue would be of any use if there were no longer anything normative and definite for anyone in their religion. In other words, the virtue of capacity for dialogue needs the virtue of steadfastness (understood not statically but dynamically). Both virtues belong together.

5. What Does Dialogue on the Basis of Steadfastness Lead To?

(a) The consequences of a dialogue rooted in faith

Those who stand in their own tradition, but at the same time are self-critically open to other traditions,

- begin with what is given and leave completely to the process of conversation and understanding what will finally emerge as a result and what can finally be said, say, on the relationship of Jesus Christ to the prophet Muhammad (to take just Christian-Muslim dialogue as an example here). This is emphatically an *a posteriori* approach;
- see the different traditions, their foundation documents and bearers of salvation, in their context and with their own status (for example, it is well known that in Islam the equivalent position to Jesus the Christ in Christianity is not occupied by Muhammad, who did not want to be a Christ, but by the Qur'an), so that a differentiated overall view of interwoven traditions becomes possible. This is a strictly historical approach, for all its anchoring in faith;
- *a priori* accept the standpoint in faith of their conversation partners and primarily expect of them unconditional readiness to listen and learn, and unlimited openness which includes a transformation of the two conversation partners in the course of a process of arriving at an understanding. This is a patiently realistic way;
- *a priori* acknowledge their own conviction of faith (Jesus is normatively and definitively the Christ) and at the same time take seriously the function, say, of Muhammad as an authentic (post-Christian) prophet - especially his 'warning' against a deviation from belief in one God in christology. This is a self-critical Christian standpoint.

(b) And in practice?

In practice this means that those who as Christians or non-Christians can adopt such a critical/self-critical basic attitude can combine for themselves a commitment of faith and readiness for understanding, religious loyalty and intellectual honesty, plurality and identity, capacity for dialogue and steadfastness. They maintain a tie with their community on which they reflect critically and at the same time attempt, not only in their own community of faith but in others, not just to reinterpret something but to change it - with a view to a growing

102

ecumenical community.

The basic attitude of true ecumenicity knows neither aggressive behaviour towards those who think otherwise nor flight from decisions. It knows neither dogmatic combativeness nor the neutralization of all standpoints. The basic attitude of true ecumenicity is that of readiness for dialogue in steadfastness: for Christians, holding firm in loyalty to the Christian cause, incorruptibly and without anxiety about reprisals. At this point some uninformed people may talk of ecumenical wishful thinking. But no thinking is denied its wishes. And anyone who thinks that all wishful thinking is *a priori* an illusion should also reflect: did not a few Catholics and Protestants, rooted in their tradition and at the same time self-critical, begin to talk together a good half century ago, in a similar wishful attitude? And precisely by remaining faithful to their own faith-communities, did they not change themselves and, in time, the two church communities? Something similar can also be hoped for, and indeed will happen, between the world religions, though over a longer space of time.

6. Capacity for Dialogue is Capacity for Peace

(a) On the way

Have I not brought out the differences between the two methods of dialogue far too sharply? Perhaps. In actual dialogue some things may be simpler, and many Christians will probably be able to assent to the following points:

- We should no longer want to tread our own Christian way, stubbornly dogmatic and uninformed about other ways, without understanding, tolerance and love for others.
- Nor should we change to other ways, disappointed about our own way and fascinated by the novelty of a new one.
- Finally, we should not simply make external additions to our old faith from what we have learned from other religions.
- Instead of this, out of an authentically Christian commitment, in constant readiness to learn, we should keep on transforming ourselves on our own way and allow ourselves to be reformed by what we learn from the other religions, so that the old faith is not destroyed, but enriched. This is what John Cobb[113] calls 'the way of

103

creative transformation', the way of Christian faith which is constantly to be ventured in ecumenical commitment. Does that confront us with a completely new task? Not at all.

(b) An epoch-making undertaking

Did not our predecessors in the ancient church, the Apologists and the Alexandrians Clement and Origen, act similarly when they encountered Neoplatonic-Stoic ways and had to work out a theology in the ecumenical paradigm of the early church? Did not Augustine and Thomas, confronted with a new Roman-Germanic world, have to do this through a process of transformation, when they had to rethink theologically the way for a Western Latin paradigm in and through the Middle Ages? Did not Luther, Calvin and the Reformers have to change when a return to the old gospel had become necessary in the great crisis of mediaeval theology and the church?

The Christian churches lost a good deal of credibility when in the paradigm of modernity, in the period of faith in science and technology, of colonialism and imperialism, there was a first intensive encounter with the world religions. In our new, post-colonialist, polycentric age, in postmodernity, it is time to take up the dialogue between Christianity and the world religions on a broad basis.

Capacity for dialogue is ultimately a virtue of capacity for peace. Precisely in that respect it is deeply human, because it is aware of the history of its failure. Where dialogues were broken off, wars broke out, in private and in public. Where dialogue failed, repressions began; the law of the jungle, the law of the more powerful, the superior, the cleverer, prevailed. Those who carry on dialogue do not shoot. And by analogy that applies to religion and the church: those who engage in dialogue will not resort to disciplining in their own church or religion, and will abhor discrimination against anyone who thinks otherwise, even heresy-hunting. Those who engage in dialogue must have the inner power and strength to sustain dialogue and where necessary to respect the standpoint of others. For one thing is certain: that impatience with dissent which is constantly breaking out all over the world, in all religions, has no understanding of the virtue of a capacity for dialogue. And yet: on this, literally on this, the whole of our spiritual and indeed physical survival will depend. For:

104

- There can be no peace among the nations without peace among the religions.
- There can be no peace among the religions without dialogue between the religions.
- There can be no dialogue between the religions without research into theological foundations. We must now reflect explicitly on this last point in a third part.

C. No Religious Peace without Religious Dialogue

Prolegomena to an analysis of the religious situation of our time

I. No Religious Dialogue without Research into Basics

What is the situation of the great religions, as human beings enter the third millennium? What must be preserved and what may be changed? What is the abiding substance of faith and what is the paradigm which changes? Where are there antagonisms and where parallels? Where are there divergences and where convergences? Where are there centres of conflict and where the beginnings of conversation? However, before we come to that there is a preliminary question to be asked.

1. A Christian Theologian on Other Religions?

(a) Appropriateness and sympathy

Can a Christian theologian write at all appropriately on other religions, for example Judaism and Islam? Or conversely, can a believing Jew or Muslim really write appropriately on Christianity? The answer is that a Jew or Muslim can write about Christianity, and a Christian about Judaism and Islam, at least as appropriately as a French person can write about Germany and a German person can write about France. May not the 'outside perspective' of the other often more easily recognize problems and opportunities than that of the insider, to whom everything is already familiar? 'Appropriately' does not mean objectively and without involvement (as a mere observer), nor does it mean arbitrarily and unobjectively (as a religious enthusiast): it means with personal commitment and therefore specifically with a particular interest in the matter. How can we understand this more precisely?

- In the face of the 'scientific' prejudices of some 'neutral' scholars in religion, it has to be stressed that objective knowledge of religious reality and subjective religious experience can supplement and enrich each other.

- In the face of the 'dogmatic' prejudices of some theologians who think in terms of norms, it has to be maintained that scientific detachment and an 'objective' description are presuppositions for a judgment which makes a 'subjective' assessment and a personal commitment.

Now for inter-religious dialogue, as I have broadly explained in Part B of this book, loyalty to one's own tradition and faith community does not exclude a sensitivity towards those of other faiths that is orientated on dialogue. On the contrary, loyalty and solidarity can come together in a critical/self-critical scientific approach which has no ideological prejudices; that is true for the comparative study of law, politics and history, as well as for the study of religion.

(b) An ecumenical research project on the religious situation of the time

In the basic attitude of a critical/self-critical scientific approach, in the coming years I want to embark on the venture of a new research project, in order to do justice to the most significant religious traditions and human communities of humankind in a contemporary way, and so serve ecumenical understanding between religions: 'No world peace without religious peace. Global analyses and perspectives on the religious situation of humankind.'[114] Here I shall sketch out briefly and justify methodologically how this can come about.

This research project will discuss with the greatest possible objectivity and at the same time spiritual involvement and sympathy the oldest of the prophetic religions, Judaism: Judaism as a religion and - to the degree that this belongs with it - the Jews as a people, indeed Judaism as a world religion of a quite distinctive kind. However, Judaism will not be investigated in isolation, as in current handbooks, introductions or histories, but in the context of a wider investigation of all three prophetic religions. It will be set against the two other Abrahamic religions, with Christianity above all, but also with Islam. So the first three studies will be devoted to the three prophetic religions. Whether it will also be possible for me to do the same thing with the religions of Indian and Chinese origin remains to be seen.

As I already observed in the introduction to this book, I am not embarking on this difficult, wide-ranging and multi-level enterprise without preparation. On the contrary, in the course of more than four decades, through lectures, conversations and colloquia, through travel and above all through scholarly publications, I have worked out the basis for myself. But whereas in earlier studies, as a Christian theologian I had to illuminate Christianity and the non-Christian religions above all from the perspective of the great classical questions (God and world, human beings and the way to salvation, church and state), in the framework of this new project the situation as it has come into being historically, the various social models and the specific tendencies in the development of these religions, will stand in the foreground: their past, present and future. Here the analyst of the times will not replace the theologian, but supplement him. At the same time I shall be concerned with urgent questions of world politics and quite personal ultimate questions of human existence.

But how - to put the question again - should a Christian theologian write appropriately about the great religions? There are already many methods in historiography, and none of them is the only correct one.[115] The libraries are full of up-to-date information on the individual religions, but to grasp this spiritually verges on the impossible.[116]

2. The Risk of Synthesis cannot be Avoided

(a) Seeing things as a whole

I myself have learned immeasurably much during my life from Christian and increasingly also from other historians, philosophers, theologians and specialists of all kinds. But with the most capable of them - heralds of inter-religious dialogue like the Jewish philosopher Martin Buber, the Canadian scholar of religions Wilfred Cantwell Smith, and the Christian theologian Raimundo Panikkar - I am of the opinion that the analysis of texts and archaeological discoveries, the enumeration of facts and dates and accounts of persons and events, is not enough for the understanding of such highly complex entities as Judaism, Christianity and Islam - not to mention the religions of Indian and Chinese origin. Therefore the specialist scholar, in particular, cannot evade the demand for synthesis.

To put it another way, it is important as far as possible to obtain a view of the whole of a religion, and indeed generally this must always be one's concern. However, the whole of a religion shows not only developments, historical sequences and dates but also structures, patterns of believing, thinking, feeling and acting. A religion is a living system of religious convictions, liturgical rites, spiritual practices and institutions of very different kinds, which develop further and which are highly complex. But how is one to get an overall view of history and the present?

(b) Historical attempts

The historical criticism of the Enlightenment had increasingly removed the basis for the theological interpretation and periodization of world history as salvation history (the development of a divine plan of salvation), as it was presented in broad outline by Augustine, Joachim of Fiore or Bossuet. Montesquieu, Gibbon, Voltaire and Condorcet had introduced modern historical research. Consequently, in the modern process of secularization a number of thinkers attempted to arrive at what they claimed to be universal laws through a systematic philosophical construction of the history of the world, culture or religion. Now, however, we know that there are no historical laws with scientific accuracy; there is no one determining factor in history. Unless we want *a priori* to run in the wrong direction, particularly if we are working towards a historical systematic analysis, we must keep clear of all historical speculations and preconceived systematizations.

II. How History Can No Longer Be Written

A global approach to world history has established itself only in the last two centuries. And if I am to give a brief methodological justification for my own approach here, we must take at least a short look at three more recent global interpretations of the history of humankind as it begins in the strict sense with the invention of writing and the high cultures.

1. Hegel's Philosophy of History

(a) A philosophy of the history of the world and of religion

It was Georg Friedrich Wilhelm Hegel who, in splendid universality and well-wrought conceptuality, worked out the first comprehensive and systematic philosophy of history.[117] Here for Hegel world history is no way a harmless harmonious development, a view which he is often accused of having taken. Hegel, who in his life had experienced the Ancien Régime, the French Revolution, the Napoleonic Wars and the subsequent restoration, was no naive believer in progress, but lived from the experiences of a deeply antagonistic society. For him world history is a slaughterhouse, the combative and dialectical stage-by-stage process of introducing and doing away with. Here each stage has its particular characteristic principle in the spirit of a people, in which the actions of individuals, even of the great individual figures of world history, are taken up and transcended; this is the spirit of the people which continually finds its way into the universal world Spirit by its rise, culmination and decline. So world history can be described as judgment on the world, and it is the philosopher who notes the judgments which have been spoken and delivered on peoples and states, their victories and defeats, their rise and decline. This is a powerful fresco of world history in context, which has had an effect even down to the present day.

But for all one's admiration for Hegel's brilliant achievement, there is no room for any historical-idealistic compulsion into a system of

112

Hegel's kind (or conversely a materialist-economic system like that of Marx and Engels[118]) in an analysis of the religious situation of the time. Let us look more closely. In his *Lectures on the Philosophy of World History,* which are valued even by opponents, Hegel treats concrete history through the great ages of the world as a powerful East-West movement of growing freedom: from the oriental world as the childhood of the human race (China, India, Persia, Western Asia and Egypt) to the Greek world as the time of its youth and the Roman world as its manhood; from there he moves finally to the Germanic world as the mature old age of humankind. All is irreversibly directed towards the final goal of history, the realization of freedom. And in all this it is striking how intensively Hegel already came to grips with the East - in contrast to the later great figures of historiography like Leopold von Ranke and Jakob Burckhardt. For Ranke, author of a sixteen-volume world history (1881-88), who established the strictly historical method in academic practice in Germany, still thinks largely in Eurocentric terms, as does Jakob Burckhardt, the admirer of the Italian Renaissance and the author of the *Reflections on History,* which were only published posthumously (1905), for whom the East was in fact bracketted off from Western history.

With his universal philosophy of history Hegel wanted to give a Christian interpretation of history, to the extent that, in his view, Christianity played the decisive role in the last world period of the Germanic peoples. That becomes even clearer when on the basis of his philosophy of world history Hegel discusses the 'philosophy of religion' and here gives an imposingly closed, deep-rooted phenomenological description and speculative interpretation of the history of religions: from the nature religions (the Godhead as a power of nature), through the religions of spiritual individuality (Judaism - Greece - Rome) to absolute religion. So he ranges from the religions of the Eskimos and Africans up to Christianity. But here at all points the same critical question arises.

(b) A logical and necessary development?

Hegel's philosophy of history had an incalculable influence on the historicization of thought generally - not least through its materialistic inversion in Marx and Engels. And Hegel represented a tremendous stimulus and challenge, in particular for historical research. Nevertheless, the German historical school (Leopold von Ranke), which was also stimulated by Hegel, unmasked Hegel's omniscient giant system as a largely speculative construction and repudiated his compulsion to form a system and his scheme of progress. Did a divine 'world Spirit' in its dialectical process of development by logical necessity constantly have to pass through particular phases or religions down the millennia of the history of the world and religion, in combat with itself? Did constantly new triples (thesis-antithesis-synthesis) have to be accomplished in order finally to arrive at the realization of self-awareness and - through Reformation and Enlightenment - complete freedom? From the nature religions through Judaism, Greece, Rome to Christianity . . . ?

For a contemporary analysis it is striking that Judaism, the 'religion of sublimity', is left behind in the process of the dialectical self-unfolding of the Spirit as an early stage: it is necessarily 'sublated' through the Greek 'religion of beauty' and the Roman 'religion of purposefulness' into Christianity as the only 'absolute religion'. And Islam? In Hegel's world-historical scheme it finds a place only at the edge of the 'Germanic Christian world': a primarily large-scale 'revolution of the East' which has long since run its course and has retreated from the field of world history into oriental leisureliness and rest.

2. Spengler's Morphology of Culture

(a) Outlines of a morphology of world history

It was then above all the German philosopher of history Oswald Spengler, born in 1880, and influenced more by Nietzsche's ideas than by Hegel's universal view of history (man as an inventive predator with a will to power), who repudiated Hegel's view of world history as a logical, continuous, progressive coming into being of the divine world Spirit in the direction of the Christian West.[119] Here according to Spengler, too, world history is to be understood not in terms of national states but of the cultures which spread beyond the nations. For he had learned from Goethe that cultures are like ensouled 'organisms', which are subject to the cyclic law of the germination, blooming and fading of plants.

And so Spengler develops the extremely learned physiognomy of eight essentially different great cultural cycles, independent of one another and shut in on themselves, the 'symbols' of which are an expression of the state of their souls. According to the cyclical law of life they were all granted a duration of around a millennium, after which they could continue to exist only as civilizations under an autocratic regime before they declined. That is true of the Babylonian, Egyptian, Indian and Chinese cultures; it is true of the Graeco-Roman, Arab and South American (Maya) cultures; and it is now also true of Western culture.

Spengler's 'Outlines of a Morphology of World History' in fact culminate - in complete contrast to Hegel's European Christian optimism at the culmination of modernity - in the 'decline of the West'. Hence the main title of his two volumes, which appeared in 1918 and 1922. And so immediately after the First World War, the downfall of the thousand-year German Empire, the collapse of the system of the state church which had been established since the Reformation, and the public collapse of bourgeois values and norms, these volumes exactly matched the mood of the time and made a tremendous impression on the mass of contemporaory intellectuals. Spengler also proved right - leaving aside other prognoses, right and wrong - in his prediction of autocracy and the subjugation of the masses at the end of the Western cycle of culture: through Communism, Fascism and National Socialism. But does all this justify his basic conception?

(b) The decline of the West?

Spengler's method of a morphology of culture has retained its place in historiography - in the face of a form of historical writing focussed entirely on the national state and politics. However, quite apart from the objections to numerous of Spengler's individual assertions, what has not stood up has been his basic conception of strictly determined developments which are to be accepted fatalistically as 'destiny'. And to this degree such a historicistic predetermining morphology of culture à la Spengler is of little help for an analysis of the religious situation.

Beyond question Spengler had a perceptive insight into the collapse of Faustian-dynamic European modernity, which had also been felt strongly by theologians like Barth and Tillich or philosophers like Buber, Bloch, Heidegger, Jaspers, Adorno and Horkheimer (not to mention other writers and artists like Thomas Mann and Hermann Hesse). And in fact since the First World War an epoch-making change has been going on, as we have constantly seen. But what is Spengler's therapy? Without doubt the historian Spengler was moving in the wrong direction when in the face of the struggle to rule the world he pleaded for the rebirth of Prussia in an authoritarian, autocratic Führer state - as a bulwark as it were against the attack of coloured peoples! Certainly Spengler, who with such convictions prepared the way for Nazism, did not ultimately become a Nazi; his aristocratic, anti-democratic disposition made him reject such a barbaric, plebeian revolution from below. But Spengler, who died in 1936, could not, and would not, think about the possibility of a postmodern epoch (which also means a polycentric, transcultural and multi-religious epoch), and certainly not about a new European community. And in understanding the cultures as 'ensouled' units of history and style incapable of communication, his physiognomy of culture overlooked the possibility of a transfer of economic and social patterns, which has meanwhile been tried so often, and in particular overlooked the indestructible power of the great religions, which extends beyond culture. Religions can themselves survive the 'decline' of an existing culture (in another or a new culture). In the face of real history there is no basis for a belief in historical 'rhythms' or 'trends' necessitated by nature on the basis of which it would then be possible to make infallible predictions.

So Spengler was wrong with his fundamental determinism, irrationality and pessimism. And he was also wrong about the two other prophetic religions. What about Islam? According to Spengler it is not really a new religion at all, but in it is to be found the 'soul of Magian (Arab) Culture - its true expression';[120] however, this has already declined before the Christian West. And Judaism? Despised and hated as a race, Jewry, 'with its ghetto and its religion, itself is in danger of disappearing': 'In the moment when the civilized methods of the European-American world cities shall have arrived at full maturity, the destiny of Jewry - at least of the Jewry in our midst (that of Russia is another problem) - will be accomplished.'[121] Accomplished?

3. Toynbee's Theory of Cycles of Civilizations

(a) Spiritual evolution in cycles

Arnold Toynbee, the British historian and philosopher of history (1889-1975), takes up both Hegel's and Spengler's ideas of a construction of world history as cultural unity, but develops it in a more moderate and milder form.[122] Without Hegelian speculation about the world Spirit in world history and without Spenglerian determinism, irrationalism and pessimism, Toynbee seeks to combine Hegel's idea of evolution with Spengler's theory of cycles. Instead of using an intuitive, evocative style like Spengler, in his monumental twelve volumes entitled *The Study of History* (1934-61), the British author seeks to present a universal- historical synopsis of the cultures in an undogmatic-empirical approach. Always starting from the historical challenge conditioned by the situation and the specific 'response' to it, unlike Spengler he wants to take positive account of the creative power of individuals and minorities inside and outside the cultural community in question (which similarly is more important for him than the state); this excludes certain prognoses for the future in a Spenglerian sense.

So Toynbee embarks on a strictly historical description of all the civilizations which ever existed: their origin, growth, decline and collapse. According to Toynbee there have been twenty-six civilizations in the barely 6000 years since the high cultures came into being, but around half of them are extinct: in addition to the Sumerian, Egyptian and Minoan civilizations there are also the Babylonian, Hittite, Near Eastern and Hellenistic civilizations and four different Central and South American civilizations, and finally Christian Orthodox (the main body and its Russian offshoot) and Western civilization.

That means that in contrast to Spengler's view, which isolates civilizations, Toynbee brings out the contacts between the civilizations (which are only relatively independent!) in both space and time. But at the same time he combines the theory of cycles with the theory of evolution: he sees the rhythm of rising and falling civilizations overlaid with the progressive spiritual development of the human race. And here the great religions (and in the final phases the universal churches as well as the universal states) are given central significance. Toynbee sees clearly that militarism and war were the graveyards of all previous cultures. Nevertheless, he did not expect the decline of the West.

117

Rather, he sees hope also for Christianity, which has an influence everywhere and has proved capable of change. However, particularly in his last creative phase, in the face of the critical world situation Toynbee saw the ecumenical opening up of Christianity to the other world religions as an extremely urgent task.[123] Indeed his view was that the twentieth century would be stamped on historical memory not for the invention of the atomic bomb but for the beginning of a serious dialogue between Christianity and Buddhism - the two most strongly opposed positions. [124]

(b) Towards a unitary religion?

Of course objections can be made to some of Toynbee's constructions. It is for experts to decide whether 'Indian civilization' (the Maurya and the Gupta empires) is to be so strongly distinguished from 'Hindu civilization' (under the Moguls and British rule) or 'Chinese civilization' (the Ch'in and Han dynasties) from Far Eastern civilization (the Mongols and the Manchu dynasty). It seems to me more correct to keep to a cultural and religious history of one people (Indian or Chinese) and here distinguish different overall constellations or paradigms rather than two civilizations.

More importantly, in the face of a possible nuclear war and the ruin of the human race which that makes possible, will the higher religions come to be bound together in a single unitary religion made up of Christian, Muslim, Hindu and Buddhist elements in the service of a single human society, as Toynbee assumed? Hardly. For nowadays a single human society and a single religion again seem further away from us than after the Second World War; globalization on one level does not exclude regionalization on another. Indeed, in view of the global 'homologization' that I already addressed in Part A, we are even confronted with the new outbreak of old ethnic and religious differences and antagonisms.

And so while we may recognize Toynbee's powerful achievement in both his historical treatment of the material and his systematic construction, his moderate empirical historical theory of cultural cycles, too, may not be adequate for an analysis of the religious situation of our time. For how does it stand with the two other prophetic religions? What about Islam? Toynbee praises Islam because it does not teach racial superiority. But he hardly believed in its revival. And Judaism? For Arnold Toynbee, who was not antisemitic, though as an anti-nationalist he was also anti- Zionist, this 'petrified religion' had 'lost its message for mankind'; it was only a cultural 'fossil' in the face of the ongoing spiritual development of mankind: 'a "fossil" of the extinct Syriac society'.[125] This and other painful remarks, which, however, are matched by positive statements about Judaism, are more than *faux pas*; rather, they betray a weakness in Toynbee's system generally, in its attempt to combine Hegel's notion of development with Spengler's theory of cycles.[126] The universal historian had an explicit antipathy to all 'claims to uniqueness', whether these appeared in Jewish, Christian or Germanic garb.

Much as we can learn even today from great figures like Hegel, Spengler and Toynbee and their enormous learning, nowadays we must take another way in assessing the religious situation of the time. What should that be? We shall be helped in surveying religion in history and in the present on the one hand by distinguishing three currents of religious systems (of Near-Eastern Semitic, Indian and Chinese origin), and on the other by a paradigm analysis which investigates changing epoch-making overall constellations in every religion (and culture).

III. Application of the Paradigm Theory to the Currents of Religious Systems

Instead of neglecting Judaism and Islam as present forces and on the other hand distinguishing three cultures within Christianity - Christian Orthodox, Russian Orthodox and Western (with the first absolutist Pope, Gregory VII, as the greatest Pope!? - criminally neglecting the thresholds of the Reformation and modernity), two things would seem important to me. Judaism, Christianity and Islam should each be understood and depicted as a whole, with subsequent distinctions of different constellations and paradigms within the one cultural history of Christianity, Judaism or Islam. The demands of the present can then be understood from the paradigms of the past, and the possibility for the future can be worked out.

1. The Significance of the Paradigm Theory

(a) The multidisciplinary study of religion

In order to do as much justice as possible to religions like Judaism, Christianity and Islam in their riches, their many levels and their many dimensions, and then at the same time to achieve profound historical perspicacity and structural transparency, an attempt must be made to overcome the often artificial division of the academic disciplines - in addition to the history, phenomenology, psychology and sociology of religion finally including philosophy and theology - and integrate different methods in order to contribute to the 'multidisciplinary study of religion' (to use Ninian Smart's[127] term) which is called for today. How can that happen in practice?

Towards the end of a long scholarly life, Mircea Eliade (1907-1986), a religious historian of truly universal learning, who was born in Rumania and then taught in Bucharest, Paris and lastly in the University of Chicago, attempted to master and structure the tremendous current of four thousand years of human religious development from the Stone Age to the present in a multi-volume *History of Religious*

Ideas.[28] It is a large-scale work, but it only avoids being antiquarian history writing if the reader is ready to be challenged existentially by it. Certainly this work by Eliade remained incomplete and shared the fate of so many great works of cultural and spiritual history, up to the *Church Dogmatics* of Karl Barth. But even so, it remains the most imposing history of the central religious ideas, conceptions of faith, myths, rites and figures - all focussed on dialectical crises over fundamentals and creative moments in each of the traditions. Here, however, chronology can only be maintained to a limited degree and the individual religions (in the accompanying diagram only the world religions) appear divided up at different points of the work.

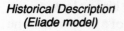
*Historical Description
(Eliade model)*

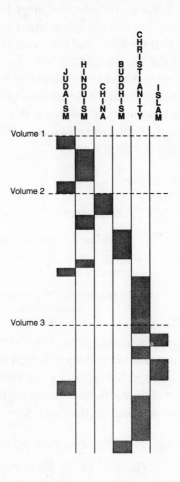

The plan adopted by Paul Tillich (1886-1965), with Karl Barth the most significant Protestant systematic theologian of this century, is quite different. In his last creative period he too taught as professor in the University of Chicago, where under the roof of the Divinity School theology and the academic study of religion are united. In contrast to Barth, the late Tillich once again allowed himself to be challenged afresh by the world of religions, and with Eliade for two years he held a joint seminar on the history of religion. On 12 October 1965 Tillich then gave a programmatic lecture in Chicago on the theme, 'The Significance of the History of Religions for the Systematic Theologian',[129] which culminated in the recognition that he, Tillich, should really rewrite his systematic theology in dialogue with the history of religions. Tillich could not know that this was to be his last lecture; ten days afterwards he died, and left behind his vision of a new systematic theology on the horizon of the world religions as something much to be desired but difficult to fulfil. After a trip to Japan he himself had proposed the systematic comparison of fundamental principles, leading ideas or leading symbols for a dialogue with Buddhism;[130] here, however, neither the overall context nor the historical development can be described adequately.

Systematic Comparison
(Tillich model)

Buddhism		**Christianity**
Nirvana	○ ◄————► ○	Eternal life
Identification with nature	○ ◄————► ○	Domination of nature
Compassion	○ ◄————► ○	Love

Having made various such comparisons in a first survey of the world religions, in a second survey I would like to attempt a new kind of method, which combines history and systematics. Who knows whether there there will then still be time enough for something like an outline of systematic theology in the context of the world religions?

(b) The historical-systematic method

Against the background of the great enterprise of Eliade and Tillich's uncompleted plan, it seems to me desirable for an analysis of the religious situation of the individual religions to combine as far as possible the narrative history of development and a topical treatment by themes. This should take place within the framework of that paradigm theory which was first developed by Thomas S.Kuhn[131] for the natural sciences but which, amidst vigorous discussion,[132] has meanwhile found application in a variety of academic disciplines.[133] I have thoroughly examined the possibility of transferring it to history,[134], tested it in an international theological symposium[135] and already made a beginning of using it.[136] So that it can be understood better, I shall first present here a substantially simplifed pattern of paradigm shifts in Christianity.

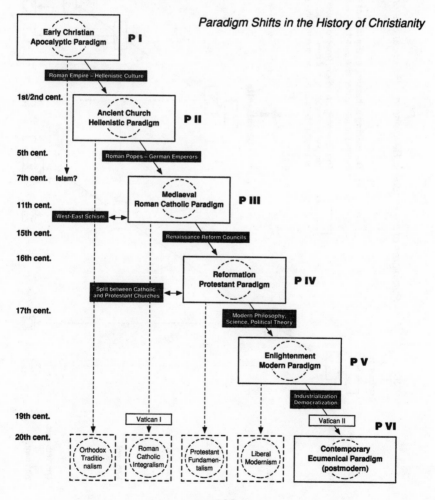

Paradigm Shifts in the History of Christianity

123

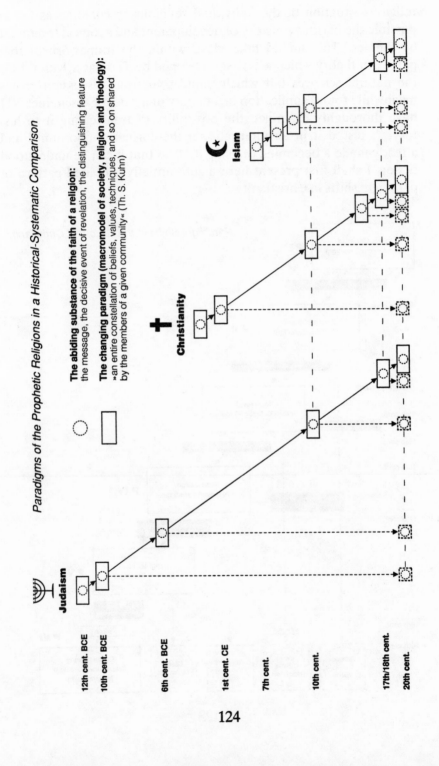

Paradigms of the Prophetic Religions in a Historical-Systematic Comparison

The abiding substance of the faith of a religion:
the message, the decisive event of revelation, the distinguishing feature

The changing paradigm (macromodel of society, religion and theology):
»an entire constellation of beliefs, values, techniques, and so on shared
by the members of a given community« (Th. S. Kuhn)

Judaism

Christianity

Islam

12th cent. BCE
10th cent. BCE
6th cent. BCE
1st cent. CE
7th cent.
10th cent.
17th/18th cent.
20th cent.

(c) A threefold goal

So we shall direct our attention - and the master emerges within limitations - less to the countless modulations and modifications in the history of the religion concerned and note, rather, the shifts in world history which still have their effects today: the epoch-making revolutions and the cultural religious constellations which follow from them and which are valid down to the present. I hope that this will make three things possible for each religion, primarily for Judaism, Christianity and Islam (see p. 115):

- a periodization which helps the survey:
  the paradigms of the past;
- a structure with a historical foundation:
  the challenges of the present;
- a prognosis which cautiously provides the agenda:
  the possibilities for the future.

2. The Same Religion in Different Paradigms

(a) Epoch-making changes

The decisive thing is to see that the great religions of the world permeate the cultures and cultural cycles and are not simply swallowed up in them. They are rather like great river systems, which can wind their way through very different cultural landscapes. Within such a religious river system each religion is to be taken seriously as a quite independent entity in its specific profile, despite all the affinities between the religions.

Here we should note that none of the great religious currents has always remained the same, though it brings water from the 'eternal'. Each has undergone such fundamental changes that one could suppose that the broad stream with many branches, flowing sluggishly through the plain, no longer had anything to do with the clear spring water of its modest beginnings. We note not only cataracts and rapids which are made to flow faster because of sudden drops or because the river bed becomes narrow, but also powerful falls, thresholds of new epochs, which result in a complete change of direction and landscape: a complete change in the overall situation. While we still have one and

125

the same religion, we now see it in a different paradigm, i.e. a different 'entire constellation of beliefs, values, techniques, and so on'.[137]

In other words, each of the great religions is not to be understood here as a static entity but as a reality which develops in a living way, which has gone through a variety of epoch-making overall constellations (macroparadigms with many meso- and microparadigms): paradigms which have partly persisted up to the present. For in contrast to the natural sciences, where the old paradigm (e.g. the Ptolemean) is replaced by the new one (the Copernican), in the sphere of religion the new (Reformation or modern) can continue alongside the old (the ancient church or the mediaeval church).[138]

So in the case of all three religions we have to ask: where are constants and variables, continuities and discontinuities, agreements and conflicts visible in their history?

(b) The persistence of rival paradigms

Here we shall be helped by the heuristic insight that down to the present day people live the same religion in different paradigms, are shaped by ongoing basic conditions and subjected to particular social mechanisms. As far as Christianity is concerned, there are still Catholics today who live spiritually in the thirteen century (contemporaneously with Thomas Aquinas, the mediaeval Popes and an absolutist church order). And there are some representatives of Eastern Orthodoxy who have remained spiritually in the fourth to fifth century (contemporaneous with the Greek church fathers). And for some Protestants the pre-Copernican constellation of the sixteenth century (with the Reformers before Copernicus and Darwin) is still normative. But what is important is that precisely this continuity, this persistence and concurrence of former religious paradigms in the present day, may be one of the main causes of conflicts within the religions and between the religions, the main cause of the different trends and parties, tensions, disputes and wars. Anyone who wants to serve peace cannot avoid a paradigm analysis.

But we might ask: if different paradigms continue in the various religions, who can be capable of surveying the whole? In view of all the religious confusion on our globe, how can a global orientation be possible?

3. The Three Great Currents of Religious Systems Today

(a) Concentration on the present world religions

The multiplicity of religions, confessions and denominations, of religious sects, groups and movements in the world today is certainly confusing, indeed disquieting. There is a combination, intermingling and opposition which can hardly be surveyed. If in a survey which is not only regional or national, but world-historical, world-wide and in this sense planetary, we want to reduce the excessive complexity which has grown up over the centuries, and in view of the current impossibility of covering it all adopt new insights, also and particularly in matters of religion, in the face of what Wilfred Cantwell Smith calls 'a new history of humankind', we will do best to keep to the great religious systems which still exist today; so many religions with their cultures have already long sunk or petered out and nowadays are only of historical interest. I shall not mention the latter here, fascinating though they can be (like the Sumerian or Egyptian religions).

That means that in the research project sketched out here I shall be concerned with:

- the religions that still exist: not those that have died out, like the religions of ancient Egypt or Mesopotamia;
- the high religions: nature or tribal religions will have to be discussed in connection with Africa and Latin America in the study on Christianity;
- the world religions: though this does not mean any devaluation of say the Sikhs, the Jains or the Bahais;
- the dynamic living reality of these religions, and not just their doctrinal structures, their systems of symbols or their organizational structures.

(b) Prophetic, mystical and wisdom religions

If we now look at the world of today and survey our globe as it were from a satellite, then, as I have indicated in different ways, in the civilized countries of this earth at present we can still distinguish three great currents of religious systems - supra-individual, international and transcultural,[139] each of which has its own genesis and morphology. In all their differences and with all their transformations and divergences we shall in particular have to consider:

127

- the religions of Semitic origin: they have a prophetic character, always begin from a contrast between God and human beings, and are predominantly involved in religious confrontation: Judaism, Christianity and Islam;[140]
- the religions of Indian origin: they are primarily supported by a basic mystical mood, tending towards unity, and are dominated more by religious inwardness: the early Indian religion of the Upanishads, Buddhism and Hinduism.[141]
- the religions in the Chinese tradition: they have a wisdom stamp and are in principle characterized by harmony: Confucianism and Taoism.[142]

Over the millennia these great religious systems have modelled the cultural landscape of this globe in a way which is older, stronger and more constant than many dynasties and empires. And just as on earth, in an incessant rhythm of change, new mountain massifs and high plateaus sporadically rise on the various continents, but great rivers, older, stronger and more constant, have continually cut their way into the rising landscape, so again and again, while constantly new social systems may erect states and ruling houses, the old great rivers of the religions can constantly find a way through - despite all the rises and falls - and shape the features of the cultivated landscape in a new way.

(c) Similar basic questions and ways to salvation

And at the same time, just as the natural river systems of this earth and the landscapes shaped by them are extremely different, but all the rivers and streams of the different continents display similar profiles and patterns of flow, obey similar regularities, cut clefts in the hills, wind over the plains, and inexorably seek a way to the sea, so it is with the religious systems of this earth. Although they are extremely different, in many respects they display similar profiles, regularities and effects. Confusingly different though all the religions are, they all respond to similar basic human questions. Where does the world and its order come from? Why are we born and why must we die? What determines the destiny of the individual and humankind? What is the foundation for moral awareness and the presence of ethical norms? And they all offer similar ways to salvation over and above their interpretation of the world: ways out of the distress, suffering and guilt

128

of existence - through meaningful and responsible action in this life - to a permanent, abiding, eternal salvation.

Now all this also means that even those who repudiate the religions will have to take them seriously as a fundamental social and existential reality; after all, they have to do with the meaning and meaninglessness of life, with human freedom and slavery, with justice and the suppression of the peoples, with war and peace in history and the present. A historical and systematic analysis of their convergences and divergences, their points of conflict and efforts at dialogue in the framework of an analysis of paradigms, is clearly called for.

IV. An Ecumenical Theology for Peace

In view of the differences and contradictoriness of religious ideas and practices, an accumulation of encyclopaedic knowledge is not enough. That can be found in any of the numerous collections of sources - not to mention the flood of specialist literature. In connection with religion, too, we suffer more than ever from an excess of information: the problem is not the collection of material, but the way in which it is assimilated and interpreted. Here - and for me in this respect Max Weber, the founder of the sociology of religion, is the model[143] - to achieve our task what we need is the power of an integral view, an eye to the essentials and a differentiated judgment. Often we need not so much a mirror, which reflects everything, as a magnifying glass, which can concentrate our gaze.

1. Understanding and Collaboration

(a) No unitary religion

Here the aim of a Christian theologian's research will certainly not just be better information for Christian colleagues, however much this is always necessary. Nor will it just be more thorough discussion with Jewish and Muslim partners in faith who have already deliberately put the same invitation to themselves. No, in addition to information and discussion there is a need to strive for a transformation, for religious understanding and collaboration, to the degree that such collaboration is necessary for peace among the religions and thus also peace among the nations. It should be stressed once again that here the postulate is not a unitary or universal religion of the kind that was already called for in vain before Toynbee by the American philosopher William E.Hocking,[144] from the Indian side by Swami Vivekananda at the Parliament of Religions in Chicago in 1893,[145] and later by Sarvepalli Radhakrishnan (India's first state president).[146] But there is a need for a contribution to peace between the religions, particularly between the prophetic religions Judaism, Christianity and Islam, which have so long been at enmity.

130

(b) A creative and concrete theology of peace

A theology for peace between Christians, Jews and Muslims should therefore first be worked out: to avoid not only any hot or cold wars (in the Near East and elsewhere), but also any pernicious self-righteousness, intolerance and rivalry. But this theology of peace must be convincing by its concreteness. For what is the use of an abstract, appellative theology of peace of the kind that is so often preached in Rome and Geneva (and sometimes also in Jerusalem)? It costs nothing because it makes all too general appeals for a readiness for understanding and a willingness for peace, and requires nothing of its own church, party or nation; so it remains voluntary, harmless and inefficient. That is no help to a creative and concrete theology of peace which

- does not shirk the labour of investigating theological foundations;
- analyses the structures of thought and conduct which have crept in;
- picks up the central differences in the religions and between the religions;
- calls for self-criticism and self-correction on all sides.

This may be thought to be an ambitious programme, and yet it is a realistic one: it is no sheer support of the *status quo* in society, state and church, no helpless admonition to show loyalty to tradition, to march on well-trodden paths, to display museum pieces. But on the other hand it is no convenient flight into a religious utopia, no completely illusory recipe, no set of impracticable suggestions or useless experiments.

So in such a research project there must be a course between the extremes, on which one neither drifts into a random pluralism nor isolates oneself with a claim to absoluteness. What I said in principle in part B of this programmatic book is now being applied here in practice: a random pluralism which accepts all religions on the same footing and presupposes that the ecumenical understanding which lies so far in the future has already achieved perfect realization, instead of working intensively for it, cannot be the goal of a realistic theology of peace. Far less, however, can the endorsement of a claim to absoluteness of Jewish, Christian or Muslim provenance, which lays absolute claim to its own truth, detached from the truth of the others, for its own religion alone. All three religions are concerned with truth, justice and salvation.

131

(c) The ecumenical horizon

The aim can only be a critical or self-critical differentiation which measures any religion critically by its own origin and by a humane ethic, without claiming it for itself. We do not arrive at peace through syncretism but through reform of ourselves; we arrive at renewal through harmony, and at self-criticism through toleration. So what is being fought for here is a theology of peace which finds the way to peace not by bracketting off the question of truth but by incorporating it and responding to it, and which above all discloses and helps to work out those conflicts and points of unrest in the world of which the religions themselves are the cause.

Such a theology for peace calls for a truly ecumenical theology which is strictly pertinent and politically and ethically relevant, and thus at the same time directed towards the future. Such an ecumenical theology claims the role neither of a self-righteous and moralizing high priest nor of an allegedly neutral supreme judge. It is as remote from any church court theology as from any uncommitted academic university theology. Despite any criticism from the church and authentic scholarship it will always be primarily concerned with the fate of those individuals and communities of faith which are affected, indeed with the future of our divided and exploited world. Theologians should not be brake-blocks, but pioneers on the way to the future.

2. Prospect

(a) The programme

World religions are primeval and contemporary, are supra-individual, international and transcultural systems, which one has to understand if one is to understand our world. Only a global, world-historical and world-wide approach will do justice to them, one which at the same time strives for two things:

- Analyses of the religious forces of the past, both the great names and the social movements, which are still effective in the present after millennia of history. That means a historical and systematic anamnesis and diagnosis;
- Forecasts from the analysis of the present of the different religious

options which are relevant for the future, both spiritually and intellectually, and socially and politically. That means a practical-ecumenical therapy and prognosis.

So for Judaism, Christianity and Islam it has to be demonstrated that:
Only if we know why it has come about ('the paradigm of the past'), can we understand our position ('the demands of the present'), and can we conjecture where everything is going ('the possibilities of the future').
So we have the past which is still present, the transitory present, and the future which is already present: the whence continues to determine the where, and the where the whither.

(b) A differentiated global survey

If the difficult task of a basic orientation of the religious situation of humankind is to succeed, I hope that:
- We shall gain a differentiated global view of the situation of religion at the threshold of a new millennium, despite all the differences between nations, regions of the world and world religions;
- We shall be able to recognize a convergence that is to be encouraged, despite the powerful and many much-splintered entities that the world religions are, extending over several thousand years, and despite the differences which are all too manifest;
- We shall see at least some fundamental and persistent constants in doctrine, practice and spirituality, despite all the striking variables in any religion: permanent factors which determine this religion through all the centuries over lands, cultures and continents, and through all paradigm changes. I hope that we shall see the same as it were eternal stars (*stellae*) by which we orientate ourselves to the present day, but which form constantly new epoch-making 'constellations'.

So the coming research project will be directed by the trust which has been grounded at length in this book:
Optimal loyalty to one's own religious faith and maximal openness to others are not exclusive.
Only in this way can we arrive at necessary mutual information, discussion and transformation.

133

The final goal of all our efforts cannot be a unitary religion; it must be an authentic peacemaking between religions.

But a last question urgently arises here: quite independently of such a research project, what can one already do for dialogue among religions? It is worth mentioning some practical possibilities, formulating some concrete imperatives.

V. Imperatives for Inter-Religious Dialogue in the Postmodern Period

In this book it has become clear from beginning to end that a new post-colonial, post-imperialistic, postmodern world constellation is in the making, and thus a polycentric world which is being bound ever closer together by new communication technologies. But at the same time this polycentric world must be a transcultural and multireligious world. In this polycentric, transcultural and multireligious world ecumenical dialogue between the world religions takes on quite new importance; for the sake of its peace this postmodern world needs more than ever the global religious understanding without which a political understanding will in the last resort no longer be possible. The slogan of the hour is therefore, 'We must begin on global religious understanding here and now!' We must advance inter-religious understanding energetically in the local, regional, national and international spheres. We must seek ecumenical understanding with all groups and at all levels. As we saw, the 'postmodern' paradigm can be described in religious terms as an ecumenical paradigm. In connection with this I would like to sketch out the specific requirements in the form of some brief ecumenical imperatives.

1. Inter-Religious Dialogue with All Groups

The decisive problems for the future with other religions are not just distant problems but problems in our midst. There are hardly any countries now without significant religious minorities (almost two million Muslims in Germany; a million Muslims and half a million of both Hindus and Sikhs in Great Britain). A new religious overview is called for; we need to seek new viable ways and strive for a new inter-religious openness, encounter and bond. In Part B of this book I began from major political questions: the civil war in Lebanon; relations between Germany on on the one hand and France and Poland on the other. From this macro-level, to end with I shall come

to the meso- and micro-levels and also address specific groups. Therefore:

(a) Politicians, businessmen, scientists

- We need people in all continents who make themselves better
  informed and orientated about the people of other lands and cultures, who take up the impulses of other religions and at the same
  time deepen the understanding and practice of their own religion.
- In particular we need men and women in politics who do not just
  see the problems of world politics which have newly arisen from the
  perspective of strategic supreme commanders or of the world market, but try to realize the conception of international peace, into
  which the longings of people in Europe and the world for reconciliation and peace, fed by religion, can be taken up.
- In addition we need men and women in business who do not just
  exploit the people of other lands and cultures - at home or abroad
  - as those who provide services, or use them in a purely economic
  function as trade partners, but rather attempt to go beyond their
  narrow economic sector and see their partners whole, as people,
  becoming sympathetic to the other human histories, cultures and
  human religions with which they have to do.
- In short, we need politicians, diplomats, business people, officials
  and also academics, not just with ever more quantitative statistical
  background knowledge but with deep historical, ethical and religious knowledge. The communication of knowledge without criteria
  of value leads people astray.

(b) Churches, theology, religious education

We need churches which despite all present tendencies towards conservatism (in the Roman Catholic, Protestant and Eastern Orthodox
spheres) do not react to new spiritual and religious challenges in a
hierarchical and bureaucratic way, but internally and externally act
close to the grassroots and are aware of problems. They should be not
centralized but organized pluralistically; not dogmatic, but attuned to
dialogue; not turned in on themselves in a self-satisfied way, but in all
the doubts of faith approaching the questions of the future self-critically and in an innovative way. In practice we need:
- a theology and theological literature which advances inter-religious

136

dialogue spiritually and intellectually in the interest of peace;
- religious education, teachers and books which serve the communication of knowledge between the religions and which understand
this work of enlightenment as practical education for peace.

(c) The different religions

We need religions which after all the hot and cold wars, after all the
co-existence which has been more divisive than peaceful, involve
themselves in constructive pro-existence and cooperation, leading to
peace in local and regional conflicts. We need a closely interwoven
network of inter-religious information, communication and co-oper-
ation. In practice all religions, as companions with equal rights, need:
- more mutual information;
- more reciprocal challenge;
- more transformation on all sides in the common quest for the
greater truth, for the mystery of the one and true God, which will
only be fully revealed, if God so wills, at the end of history.

2. Inter-Religious Dialogue at All Levels

I am not calling for an inter-religious dialogue at all levels and in all
forms for its own sake, as an end in itself, but for the sake of individuals, churches and religions, for their reconciliation, as this was con-
vincingly worked out by the Harvard specialist in religions, Diana
L.Eck, in her report for the World Council of Churches in Potsdam in
1986.[147] Therefore:

(a) Unofficial and official dialogues

- We need not only religious conferences and gatherings on the model
of the 'World Conference of the Religions for Peace', but also the
most intensive institutional contacts and bilateral relationships
(World Council of Churches, Vatican Council for Inter-religious
Dialogue, national church organizations, international Jewish,
Muslim and Buddhist associations).
- Even more, we need local and regional inter-religious base groups
and working parties which discuss and remove problems where they
arise, and investigate and realize possibilities for practical collaboration.

137

(b) Scientific and spiritual dialogue

– We need a more intensive philosophical and theological dialogue of theologians and specialists in religion which takes religious plurality seriously in theological terms, accepts the challenge of the other religions, and investigates their significance for each person's own religion (Christian-Jewish and Christian-Buddhist dialogue are models for this).
– But at the same time we need the spiritual dialogue of religious communities, of monks, nuns and laity, who are silent, meditate and reflect together and are concerned with a deepening of the spiritual life, and the questions of a spirituality for our time.

(c) Everyday dialogue

Even more, we need everyday dialogue of all the people of different religions who meet and discuss daily and hourly all over the world on all possible occasions: in mixed marriages and shared social projects, on religious festivals or in political initiatives, all over the place, where in questions great and small the religions constantly interact in a quite practical way. So in quite specific terms we need:
– external dialogue of those who live in the same street or in the same village, work in the same factory or study at the same university;
– internal dialogue, the discussion that goes on in ourselves, in our heads and hearts, whenever we encounter strangers, a person or a book, whenever for example Christians hear something from the Qur'an or Muslims something from the Gospels.[148]

The implication of the many levels of interreligious dialogue is that not only are good will and an open attitude necessary at all levels, but - on each level - also solid knowledge. But this is still often lacking - not least at the scholarly and theological level, where the problems of foundations in particular are still worked on all too little. Therefore the programme which guides us and which comes together as one may be summed up once again in three basic statements:
- no human life together without a world ethic for the nations;
- no peace among the nations without peace among the religions;
- no peace among the religions without dialogue among the religions.

138

Notes

1. Cf. Hans Küng (in chronological order)
'The World Religions in God's Plan of Salvation' in *Christian Revelation and the World's Religions* (1965) ed J. Neuner, London 1967
The Church (1967), London and New York 1968 (cited below as *Church*), especially D II 2: 'No Salvation Outside the Church?'
The Incarnation of God. An Introduction to Hegel's Theological Thought as a Prolegomena to a Future Christology (1970), Edinburgh 1987 (cited below as IG)
On Being a Christian (1974), London and New York 1976 (cited below as OBC), especially A III: 'The Challenge of the World Religions'
Does God Exist? An Answer for Today (1978), London and New York 1980 (cited below as DGE), especially G I: 'The God of the Non-Christian Religions'
Eternal Life? (^{2}1982), London and New York 1984 (cited below as EL)
(with J.van Ess, H. von Stietencron and H.Bechert), *Christianity and the World Religions. Paths of Dialogue with Islam, Hinduism, and Buddhism* (1984), London and New York 1985 (cited below as CWR)
(with W.Jens), *Dichtung und Religion. Pascal, Gryphius, Lessing, Hölderlin, Novalis, Kierkegaard, Dostojewski, Kafka*, Munich 1985 (cited below as DR)
Theology for the Third Millenium, An Ecumenical View (1987), New York 1988
Theologie im Aufbruch. Eine ökumenische Grundlegung, Munich 1987 (cited below as TM)
(with J.Ching), *Christianity and Chinese Religions* (1988), New York 1989 (cited below as CR)
(with Walter Jens), *Anwälte der Humanität. Thomas Mann, Hermann Hesse, Heinrich Böll*, Munich 1989 (cited below as AH)
Reforming the Church Today, Edinburgh and NewYork 1990.
2. Cf. especially CWR and CR.
3. Cf. especially IG, OBC, DGE, EL.
4. Cf. especially TA.
5. They come from the preparatory document for the World Assembly of the Christian Churches in Seoul 1990, *Justice, Peace and the Integrity of Creation*, Seoul, Korea, 5-13 March 1990.
6. For the overall problem, the terminology, history and content of which are extremely confusing, cf. the various interpretations of postmodernity in W.Welsch (ed.), *Wege aus der Moderne. Schlüsseltexte der Postmoderne-Dis-*

kussion, Weinheim 1988.

7. Cf. J.-F.Lyotard, *La condition postmoderne,* Paris 1979. At least in this programmatic work (in other publications he later takes a different course) Lyotard gives a chronologically correct definition of postmodernity as 'the state of culture after the transformations which the rules of the games of science, literature and the arts have undergone since the end of the nineteenth century' (13). Wolfgang Welsch's own analysis (*Unsere postmoderne Moderne,* Weinheim [2]1988) provides a wide range of information and an acute analysis, but his solution begins too quickly, passes over the epoch-making shift in our century which I shall go on to analyse, and narrows down the broad spectrum of postmodern conceptions and outlines to the category of 'radically pluralist' (39) by declaring that other concepts are 'deviations'. Modernity, postmodernity or postmodern modernity? In the whole discussion, both in the German and the French philosophers (influenced by Nietzsche and Heidegger) one must beware of vaguenesses, ambiguities and false profundity which would justify the verdict of Karl Popper, who derives all this from Hegel's dialectic: 'This way of speaking is virtually *de rigueur* in wide areas of German literature and German science, particularly in the social sciences and above all of course also in German philosophy. And the result of that is that when someone speaks clearly and simply, it is already assumed: "Well, yes, what he says is very fine and correct - but this man really does not get down to the really great and significant depths" ' (*Die Welt,* 23 February 1990).

8. A look at art may show further depths of the problem. Art, more dependent than, say, philosophy, the natural sciences or constitutional theory on its patrons in state and church, had a belated start in the modern period - only after the end of the Ancien Régime around 1800. But once the breakthrough was made with impressionism - in painting, sculpture, architecture and music - it reached its modern climax ('classical modernity') uncannily quickly, was finally drawn into the crisis of modernity and is now tentatively looking for postmodern ways. The important thing would be, despite all the time-warps in the various sectors, to have as broad as possible a conspectus of the various sectors, areas, subject fields and spheres of life in order to arrive at an overall picture of our time. I have demonstrated the extent to which the First World War was experienced as the decisive epoch-making change, from theology to literature, on the one hand by Karl Barth ('Karl Barth und die katholische Theologie', in *Theologische Literaturzeitung* 112, 1987, 561-78) and on the other by Thomas Mann and Hermann Hesse (cf. AH).

9. Significantly, 'postmodern' as a term for an epoch in world history appears in connection with Friedrich Nietzsche, that most acute critic of modernity, in the cultural crisis of the First World War (R.Pannwitz, *Die Krisis der europäischer Kultur,* Nuremberg 1917, II, 64). Arnold Toynbee used it in 1947 for the contemporary epoch of Western culture which for him begins even before the First World War with the transition from the politics

of the national state to global interaction (the shorter version of A.Toynbee's great work, *A Study of History*, abridgment of Volumes I-VI, ed D.C.Somervell, Oxford 1947, 39): 'There is ample reason for supposing that we have recently passed into a New chapter: . . . "Post-Modern"?, 1875-?'. North American literary critics and architects took over the term from Toynbee, but with a now completely new restricted and lame sense. Cf.A.Wellmer, *Zur Dialektik von Moderne und Postmoderne*, Frankfurt 1985; A.Huyssen and K.R.Scherpe (eds.), *Postmoderne. Zeichen eines kulturellen Wandels*, Hamburg 1986; P.Kemper (ed.), *'Postmoderne' oder Der Kampf um die Zukunft. Kontroverse in Wissenschaft, Kunst und Gesellschaft*, Frankfurt 1988.

10. For a balanced assessment of Karl Marx see DGE, C II: 'God - a consolation serving vested interests? Karl Marx'.

11. Even more suspicious than the frauds of the leading Wall Street financiers like Dennis Levine, Ivan Boesky and above all the junk-bond pioneer Michael Milken (in this era perhaps the most powerful man in the American financial world), which ran into hundreds of millions of dollars, is the way in which so many banks, businesses and media admired, covered up and even unrestrainedly joined in their unscrupulous activites. If one has taught for several semesters in American universities during the 1980s, one knows how many Americans disapproved of these consequences of 'Reaganomics'.

12. *Time* Magazine, 1 January 1990: 'Freed From Greed? The past decade brought growth, avarice and an anything-goes attitude. But the '90s will be a time for the U.S. to fix up, clean up and pay up' (58-60). In America people are now talking of a new 'age of limits'.

13. Cf. P.Kennedy, *The Rise and Fall of the Great Powers*, London and New York 1987.

14. P.Volcker, 'American Leadership: Still Possible, Still Needed', in *International Herald Tribune*, 19 December 1989. The American work written jointly by the economist H.E.Daly and the Protestant theologian John B.Cobb with the programmatic title *For the Common Good. Redirecting the Economy toward Community, the Environment, and a Sustainable Future*, Boston 1989, appeared opportunely. Referring to the 'solidarism' of the Catholic theologian and economist Heinrich Pesch, they argue for a 'paradigm shift in economics'.

15. K.van Wolferen, *The Enigma of Japanese Power*, London and New York 1989. As with Germany, the repression of guilt for the war and war crimes for almost fifty years after the end of the war will not help Japan much. The most recent symptoms of repression (in 1990) are: the assassination attempt by a right-wing nationalist on the brave mayor of Nagasaki, Shitoshi Motoshima, who on the occasion of the death of emperor Hirohito publicly affirmed his complicity in the misery of war; this also outraged many Japanese. Also the rejection by the mayor of Hiroshima of an application, on an initiative

of the citizens, for the erection of an 'Aggressors' Corner' in the Hiroshima Peace Museum (which is now to be renovated at a cost of millions). In the museum I saw a collection down to the tiniest detail of the terrifying relics of the atom bombing, but not the slightest mention of the Japanese wars of aggression against Korea, China, South East Asia and the United States which had preceded it.

16. Cf. M.Frank, 'Die Rettung des Individuellen. Zwei Jahrhunderte Rationalitäts-Kritik und ihre "postmoderne" Überbeitung', *Schwäbisches Tagblatt*, 6 June 1987: 'Today - or rather in our days - what would have been incredible from the perspective of the seventeenth and eighteenth century has happened, that "reason/rationality" itself and as such has been hauled to judgment and has to answer the question of its legitimacy. To question the legitimacy of rationality is nothing less than to put under suspicion that authority which had long given legitimacy on the grounds that it was itself in need of legitimation.' Frank rightly goes on to make Romanticism already an opponent of the concept of reason and the state in the Enlightenment. 'The emancipatory mission of the Enlightenment turned into a new cult of rationality, as soon as rationality declared itself to be autonomous, and thus neglected to reflect on the synthetic actions in which it is grounded. A process of reason left to itself is like a machine which goes by itself, the functioning of which is no longer under the control of a purpose. Because analytic rationality, taken to extremes, rejects the ideas of purposefulness and justification by "ideas", with the idea of the untenability of positivities, at the same time it does away with the notion of the possibility of legitimation as such ("undermines itself to the point of self-annihilation" are Friedrich Schlegel's own words).'

17. Cf.F.Capra, *The Turning Point,* New York and London 1982. As a physicist and philosopher Capra attacks the physical-mechanistic world-view of modernity (Descartes, Newton, Darwin) with all its far-reaching consequences and goes on to call for another perception of the world: not linear, but complex; not in the straight lines and curves of statistics, but in networks and curves. Qualitative values must take the place of quantitative measurement; for the world is more than the sum of its parts.

18. Cf. I.Prigogine and I.Stengers, *La Nouvelle Alliance. Métamorphose de la science*, Paris 1979.

19. Cf. D.Mieth, 'Moral der Zukunft - Zukunft der Moral?', in *Kirche in der Zeit. Walter Kasper zur Bischofsweihe*, ed. H.J.Vogt, Munich 1990, 198-223.

20. N.Wiener, *The Human Use of Human Beings. Cybernetics and Society,* New York 1950.

21. Cf. D.Riesman, 'Leisure and Work in Post-Industrial Society', in *Mass Leisure*, ed. E.Larrabee and R.Meyersohn, Glencoe 1958, 363-85.

22. Cf. D.Bell, *The Coming of Post-Industrial Society. A Venture in Social Forecasting*, New York 1973, esp.29-56, 374-6; A.Touraine, *La société post-*

industrielle, Paris 1969 (a 1968 analysis of the contradiction between business mechanisms and social organization in the light of the student movement, in connection with a 'programmed society').

23. Cf. P.Oertli-Cajacob (ed.), *Innovation statt Resignation. 35 Perspektiven für eine neue Zeit*, Berne 1989, Part V: 'Einblick, Überblick, Ausblick', 351-72.

24. A proposal made in the American Senate to save just 1% of the defence budget (which in 1989 was 125 billion dollars) for the reconstruction of Eastern Europe represented 1,250 million dollars in immediately available resources.

25. Cf. J.Naisbitt and P.Aburdene, *Megatrends 2000. Ten New Directions for the 1990s*, New York 1990. In chapter 8, 'The Age of Biology' - before the chapter on 'The Revival of the Religions' which brings together a great variety of data and curiosities (all from the USA) - one reads with amusement a thesis like this, printed in bold type: 'Philosophers and theologians - for centuries chronically underemployed - are now as sought-after and desired as information theorists' (339). For *Megatrends 2000* see the justified criticism by L.Niethammer, 'Erdbeertunke des Optimismus', *Der Spiegel* 16, 1990, 237-41.

26. For the concept of the paradigm cf. DGE (1978!), A III.1; TA, B II-IV. 'Paradigm shift' comes from the American historican of science Thomas S.Kuhn, *The Structure of Scientific Revolutions*, Chicago 1962; it was first investigated systematically and theoretically for the discovery of truth in the sphere of the natural sciences. It does not mean the alteration of a method or a theory but the change of an 'entire constellation of beliefs, values, techniques, and so on shared by the members of a given community' (175). In the context of religion, paradigm shift means a change in the whole constellation, the basic model, basic framework by which human beings perceive themselves, society, the world and God.

When transferred from the history of science to history generally and the history of Christianity in particular, the term 'paradigm shift' does not just denote some swing of the pendulum or wave, nor just a change of mood or a particular political change. Rather, it means a change in the view of things generally which is both fundamental and long-term, and finally is perceived widely: a shift in the macroparadigm, which always includes many meso- and microparadigms. What is decisive for the replacement of a paradigm is the breakthrough of many individual innovative signals of the past (in pioneering thinkers, critical groups of all kinds which are before their time, for example postmoderns 'avant la lettre'), so that it becomes an overall trend which is perceived by the broader masses. The decisive factor is not that individual indicators of the crisis and the shift were 'already there' but what has really 'made history'.

27. On this see K.-H.Hillmann, *Wertwandel. Zur Frage soziokultureller Voraussetzungen alternativer Lebensformen*, Darmstadt [2]1989. The thematic volume of the international journal *Concilium*, 191, 1987, *Changing Values*

and Virtues, edited by D.Mieth and J.Pohier, is concerned throughout with contemporary ethical problems.

28. Cf. O.Weggel, *Die Asiaten,* Munich 1989, 38-53: the real difference from the West is totality or harmony (in accord with the human environment, nature, what lies beyond the senses).

29. In his final conclusions J.-F.Lyotard writes polemically - it seems to me wrongly - against the discursive ethics of Jürgen Habermas, who would like to solve the problem of legitimation by a universal consensus: 'Consensus has become an obsolete and suspect value, but not justice. So we must arrive at an idea and a praxis of justice which is not tied to that of justice' (op.cit., 190). On this cf. M.Frank, *Die Grenzen der Verständigung. Ein Geistergespräch zwischen Lyotard und Habermas,* Frankfurt 1988.

30. W.Welsch, *Unsere postmoderne Moderne,* Weinheim ²1988, 4f.; cf. 5, 'pluralism in principle'. At the second Bertelsmann Colloquium on 17/18 February 1989, 'The Future of Basic Values', the Swiss ethicist Walther C.Zimmerli (Bamberg) similarly marked the opposite point of view to the theses of Welsch, which were also presented there: 'One of the category errors which contributes to the rise of the present defeatism over ethics is the "confusion of the levels of unity and multiplicity". This consists in the assumption that unity and multiplicity exclude each other, in that the plurality of value systems does not allow the unity of a consensus. However, precisely the opposite is the case... The plurality of first-order conceptions of value not only allows a consensus at a second level (that plurality may be allowed), but virtually presupposes it. A further category error which is connected with this, and can be found no less frequently, is the confusion of relativity and ethical relativism: it indeed follows from the fact that in a pluralistic society a variety of notions of value evidently coexist synchronously and replace one another diachronically that all notions of value have validity only relative to the system in which they belong. But that means that they must have absolute validity within this value system. Ethical relativism (which would be a contradiction in itself) does not follow from ethical relativity (which is a fact).'

31. Cf. R.Spaemann, 'Ende der Modernität?', in *Moderne oder Postmoderne? Zur Signatur des gegenwärtigen Zeitalters,* ed. P.Koslowski, R.Spaemann and R.Löw, Weinheim 1986, 19-40.

32. Cf. P.Koslowski, 'Die Baustellen der Postmoderne - Wider den Vollendungszwang der Moderne', in ibid., 1-16: 9. Koslowski's not unjustified critiicsm of modernity suffers from a vague historical definition of the concept of modernity, which should already include the Reformation, the Counter-Reformation and baroque. His clearly premodern 'essentialism in art and philosophy' (11), taking 'the legacy of antiquity and the Middle Ages' as an example, does not become 'postmodern' as a result of his desire to avoid academism and elitism.

33. In a clear-sighted analysis in the American *National Catholic Reporter*

of 13 April 1990, the British theologian and Vaticanologist P.Hebblethwaite has analysed the anxieties of the Pope over a secularization of Europe and even Poland and stressed that the premodern vision of this Pope will soon no longer have any visual model, because culturally Western Europe is not looking to Eastern Europe, but Eastern Europe to Western Europe: 'So while John Paul might broadly welcome the political consequences of the events, their religious consequences are less encouraging. If Poland, because of the changed circumstances, can no longer provide a model for the church, then what country can?' For the messianic sense of mission which in all probability is the greatest strength of the Polish Pope, but perhaps also his greatest weakness (a lack of self-criticism), see R.Modras, 'Ein Mann der Widersprüche? Die frühen Schriften des Karel Wojtyla', in N.Greinacher and H.Küng, *Katholische Kirche - Wohin? Wider den Verrat am Konzil*, Munich 1986, 225-39.

34. On this see T.Meyer, *Fundamentalismus. Aufstand gegen die Moderne*, Hamburg 1989; id. (ed.), *Fundamentalismus in der modernen Welt. Die Internationale der Unvernunft*, Frankfurt 1989; J.Niewiandomski (ed.), *Eindeutige Antworten? Fundamentalistische Versuchung in Religion und Gesellschaft*, Thaur 1988. In a model example of historical writing orientated on the social sciences, U.Altermatt, a historian at the University of Fribourg, Switzerland, in his *Katholizismus und Moderne. Zur Sozial- und Mentalitätsgeschichte der Schweizer Katholiken im 19. und 20. Jahrhundert*, Zurich 1989, gives an account of the problems of resistance and adaptation to modernity which still shape the behaviour of Catholics to the present day.

In the face of reactionary trends and growing criticism of the Roman course from the Catholic centre, I have documented and systematically summarized my own position in the church, which has been attacked over the past three decades, in *Reforming the Church Today*, Edinburgh and New York 1990.

35. I feel endorsed in this definition of postmodernity by the recent book of D.R.Griffin, *God and Religion in the Postmodern World. Essays in Postmodern Theology*, Albany, NY 1989. Griffin speaks of 'constructive postmodernism' to distinguish it from antimodernism and ultramodernism. 'This postmodernity seeks to overcome the modern worldview not through the elimination of the possibility of worldviews generally, but through the construction of a postmodern worldview by means of the revision of modern presuppositions and traditional concepts. This constructive or renewed postmodernism implies a new unity of scientific, ethical, aesthetic and traditional concepts. It does not reject science as such, but just that scientism in which only the data of modern science is allowed to contribute to the construction of our worldview' (x). With all this Griffin is aiming at 'postmodern persons' with a 'postmodern spirituality' with a view to a 'postmodern society' and a 'postmodern world order'. Most recently of all, D.Sölle, *Thinking about God. An Introduction to Theology*, London and Philadelphia 1990, has taken over

145

elements of my analysis of theological paradigms, though without, it seems, having herself mastered the necessary basic literature in the theory of science. Thus for her (7) the definition of paradigm does not come directly from Kuhn's work, as I have indicated, but from my article. On p.21 she reprints my schema on Reformation theology as her own without giving any sources (cf. TA, 230). All this would not be so bad if she did not seek to press the whole of the theology of the second millennium into a scheme which looks suspiciously ideological: orthodox (including K.Barth?), liberal (including R.Bultmann and P.Tillich?) and 'radical' ('only liberation theological minorities'?). She hardly does justice to the complex postmodern situation with this historically inaccurate schema which systematizes superficially.

36. Cf. A.MacIntyre, *After Virtue. A Study in Moral Theory*, London and Notre Dame 1981. The all-embracing cultural crisis of modernity rests on a moral crisis which MacIntyre, however (doubtless under the influence of the American development depicted at the beginning), sees in exclusively negative terms in abrupt cultural pessimism: 'We possess indeed simulacra of morality, we continue to use many of the key expressions. But we have - very largely, if not entirely - lost our comprehension, both theoretical and practical, of morality' (2).

37. According to MacIntyre even the philosophy dominant at present fails over the present modern complex of problems: 'In the real world the dominant philosophies of the present, analytical or phenomenological, will be . . . powerless to detect the disorders of moral thought and practice' (ibid.).

38. Cf. J.Mittelstrass, 'Auf dem Wege zu einer Reparaturethik?', in J.-P.Wils and D.Mieth (eds.), *Ethik ohne Chance? Erkundungen im technologischen Zeitalter*, Tübingen 1989, 89-108 (in which there are also illuminating scientific contributions by M.Wolff, G.Mack and M.Schramm, and philosophical ones by W.C.Zimmerli and O.Höffe).

39. J.Rawls, *A Theory of Justice*, Cambridge, Mass. 1971. Over against the utilitarian ethics (of Hume, Adam Smith, Bentham and Mill) dominant in the Anglo-American sphere the Harvard philosopher puts forward a theory of justice (as fairness) which is built on the theory of the social contract in Locke, Rousseau and above all Kant, and which is supposed to prove to be 'the best moral foundation for a democratic society' (12). Rawls begins from two basic definitions of justice: 'Everyone shall have equal rights to the most extensive system of equal basic freedoms which is compatible with the same system for all others. 2. Social and economic equalities are to be shaped in such a way that (a) it is reasonably to be expected that they serve everyone's advantage and (b) that they are associated with positions and offices which are open to anyone' (81). For a critical assessment cf. O.Höffe (ed.), *Theorie-Diskussion. Über John Rawls' Theorie der Gerechtigkeit*, Frankfurt 1977; H.Bielefeldt, *Neuzeitliches Freiheitsrecht und politische Gerechtigkeit. Perspektiven der Gesellschaftsvertragstheorien*, Würzburg 1990.

146

40. Bert Musschenga, an ethicist at the Free University of Amsterdam, has drawn my attention to these important aspects of dynamic consensus-finding. Lectures and discussions at various Dutch universities have provided me with much stimulation.

41. Cf. E.G.Tannis, *Alternative Dispute Resolution that Works*, North York, Canada 1989.

42. M.Weber, 'Politik als Beruf', in *Gesammelte politische Schriften*, Tübingen 1958, 505-60: quotation 559.

43. H.Jonas, *Das Prinzip Verantwortung. Versuch einer Ethik für die technologische Zivilisation*, Frankfurt am Main 1984; id., *Technik, Medizin und Ethik. Zur Praxis des Prinzips Verantwortung*, Frankfurt 1987.

44. On this see E.Laszlo, *Design for Destiny,* New York 1989.

45. P.Drucker, 'Facing the "New and Dynamic"', *Time* Magazine, 22 January 1990.

46. R.Müller, 'Führung 2000: Kapital in High Tech, Vertrauen in Mitarbeiter investieren', in *io Management Zeitschrift* 59, 1990, 1.

47. K.Bleicher, *Chancen für Europas Zukunft. Führung als internationaler Wettbewerbsfaktor*, Frankfurt 1989, 218.

48. For the problems of the institutionalization of ethics see R.Löw, 'Brauchen wir eine neue Ethik?', in *Universitas 1990*, 291- 6. For the institution of referenda cf. G.Altner, 'Präventionsprinzip und Ethik: Was ist zu tun?', *Universitas* 1989, 373-84.

49. P.Ulrich, *ordinarius* in the first chair of business ethics at a German-speaking business college (St Gallen), is therefore right in observing that the 'moral of history' consists in the insight that 'the value-conscious quality of business policy represents as important a presupposition of success in business as the quality of business strategies and executive management . . . to this degree a realistic business ethic is concerned with the central question how the institutionalized "Sachlogik" of our economic system can be reconciled methodically with contemporary ethical and practical claims' (*Schweizerischer Bankverein*, Der Monat 3, 89, 7f.).

50. *International Herald Tribune*, 12 January 1990.

51. E.Draper, *Psychiatry and Pastoral Care,* Philadelphia [2]1970, 117.

52. In these paragraphs there is also an implicit answer to the Paris sociologist Alfred Grosser, with whom I was able to have so much stimulating discussion above all in connection with the television series 'Baden-Badener-Disput' (1989/90). For all his scepticism about a closed moral system, Grosser resolutely defends the significance of ethical values and criteria for politics, and also for politology and sociology (no diagnosis of society without ethical points of references like truth, freedom and justice!) - but he does all this while explicitly repudiating a religious confession. Cf. A.Grosser, *Au nom de quoi? A la recherche d'une éthique politique,* Paris 1969.

53. The problems of a morality without belief in God are broadly developed

147

in DGE Part E, 'Yes to reality - alternative to nihilism'.

54. H.Markl, 'Vom Sinn des Wissens. Auch die Genetik ist keine Wissenschaft im "wertfreien" Raum', *Die Zeit*, 8 September 1989.

55. Cf.M.Horkheimer and T.W.Adorno, *Dialectic of Enlightenment*, London 1966.

56. Cf. K.-O.Apel, *Diskurs und Verantwortung. Das Problem des Übergangs zur postkonventionellen Moral*, Frankfurt 1988.

57. J.Habermas, *Die Neue Unübersichtlichkeit*, Kleine Politische Schriften V, Frankfurt 1985; id., *Theory of Communicative Action* (three vols), Oxford 1985-9; id., *Moralbewusstsein und kommunikatives Handeln*, Frankfurt 1983, ³1988; id., *Philosophical Discourse of Modernity*, Oxford 1988.

58. Cf. R.Bubner, *Handlung, Sprache und Vernunft. Grundbegriffe praktischer Philosophie*, Frankfurt ²1982: id., *Geschichtsprozesse und Handlungsnormen. Untersuchungen zur praktischen Philosophie*, Frankfurt 1984.

59. Cf. E.Tugendhat, *Probleme der Ethik*, Stuttgart 1984, who speaks with welcome openness: 'In the last thirty years people have again become intensively preoccupied with them (the basic questions of ethics), and in the last fifteen years also in Germany. Nevertheless, so far no one has arrived at any convincing answers' (3). In connection with his own suggestion for a solution, in the end he confesses: 'So we still await a satisfactory grounding of morality of mutual respect' (176).

60. MacIntyre, *After Virtue* (n.36), notes a failure of modern moral philosophy which builds on the presuppositions of the secularist Enlightenment; and as we cannot yet expect a moral accord in the present pluralist society, he calls on the one hand for justice and law to suppress social conflicts and on the other hand for recourse to the Aristotelian doctrine of virtue, which is orientated on individual ethics.

61. Cf.R.Rorty, *Consequences of Pragmatism, Essays 1972-1980*, Minneapolis 1982; id., *Contingency, Irony, and Solidarity*, Cambridge 1989. The author, whose background is American pragmatism, and who dreams of a 'post-religious' and 'post-metaphysical' culture - both of which are 'desirable' (*Consequences*, 15) - himself manifestly demonstrates how with a good deal of theoretical philosophical effort one can arrive at quite trivial results. For Rorty, the epoch-making fact is that 'for the first time people in large numbers are capable of separating two questions: "Do you believe and wish what I believe and wish" and "Are you suffering?" '(*Consequences*, 320). In view of a world war with 55 million dead, including 6 million gassed Jews, one would be glad to hear a serious comment from a philosopher in favour not of the dedication of countless people to a 'humankind as such' (which is now truly an abstract) but of the human rights of those who are quite specifically without rights and suffering endlessly throughout the world, who can probably make little of the 'universal irony' of such a 'liberal and ironist'.

62. Cf. M.Foucault, *Madness and Civilization*, London 1961; *The History*

148

of Sexuality, Vols I-III, London and New York 1981ff., who advocates a morality of 'souci de soi', 'self-concern', the self-realization of the individual in a splendid life-style - against any generally valid morality. Similarly Lyotard, *La condition postmoderne* (n.7). For criticism of this 'contemporary rebellion against the presumption of universal principles - especially those of morality', cf. Apel, *Diskurs und Verantwortung* (n.56), 154-78.

63. I have been helped to arrive at these insights especially through conversation with Rüdiger Bubner, my colleague in the philosophical faculty of the University of Tübingen. One can agree with his suspicions of a 'practical reason with regional limitations' without - in the age of human rights - giving up the quest for global connections and norms which are universally valid. However, nowadays one can hardly act correctly locally without thinking globally. So the historical character of all norms and a possible universal validity are not mutually exclusive, as Bubner also confirms: 'But in the meantime one can be aware that the unresolved questions directed at the heart of modernity are part of the historicity of those norms which have not only to be put forward rationally but also proved in life. Norms which concern everyone and in fact are accepted by all, which do justice to the subject and precisely in so doing shape the whole of a community, necessarily form historical configurations' (*Handlung* [n.58], 316). I recall with gratitude an interdisciplinary colloquium at our university on the theme 'Where do we Stand Today?' which I held in the winter semester of 1989/90 with Rüdiger Bubner, Manfred Frank and Dieter Langewiesche. On this see the articles by the three authors in the volume edited by J.Schmidt, *Aufklärung und Gegenaufklärung in der europäischen Literatur, Philosophie und Politik von der Antike bis zur Gegenwart*, Darmstadt 1989. For the problems of liberalism cf. D.Langenwiesche, *Liberalismus in Deutschland*, Frankfurt am Main 1988. For the state of religion before 1918 cf. T.Nipperdey, *Religion im Umbruch. Deutschland 1870-1918*, Munich 1988.

64. S.Freud, letter to J.J.Putnam of 8 July 1915, quoted in Ernest Jones, *Sigmund Freud. Life and Work*, II, *The Years of Maturity, 1901-19*, London 1967, 465.

65. Cf. A.Peccei (ed.), *No Limits to Learning: Bridging the Human Gap*, Oxford 1979.

66. J.Habermas, *Nachmetaphysisches Denken. Philosophische Aufsätze*, Frankfurt 1988.

67. Cf.M.Frank, 'Religionsstiftung im Dienste der Idee? Die "Neue Mythologie" der Romantik', in *Was aber (bleibet) stiften die Dichter? Zur Dichter-Theologie der Goethezeit*, ed. G. vom Hofe, P.Pfaff and H.Timm, Munich 1986, 121-37: 'One of the striking phenomena of our cultural and social present is the fact that the question of the mythical and quite universal, of the religious dimension not only of poetry but of life in general, has again acquired an interest which now can no longer be overlooked . . . Of social life itself, I am

saying, and by that I mean that society, the totality of the relationships between the members of a state community, its so-called "crisis of meaning", is increasingly suing in categories which are taken from religious language. People say that we lack a last obligation to which politics could refer, especially in the Western industrial nations, so that their citizens could regard them as justifiable' (121f.). Frank takes up the criticism already expressed by the early Romantics of the way in which the rationality of the Enlightenment takes apart, dissolves and dismounts, and so pleads for a new mythology: *Der kommende Gott. Vorlesungen über die Neue Mythologie I,* Frankfurt 1982; id., *Gott im Exil, Vorlesungen über die Neue Mythologie II,* Frankfurt 1988. However, it seems to me that anyone who in a society which has become atomized and myth-less will not be content on the one hand with the aestheticism of a Rilke, George or Thomas Mann in their desire to restore poetry as a modern myth, or on the other hand with the political fantasies of the Nietzschean 'artist politician' (in which Hitler believed that he could recognize himself) or Rosenberg's *Myth of the Twentieth Century* will have to progress from the new mythology to the new religious feeling or religion. For Thomas Mann's understanding of myth and religious feeling in particular, cf.AH.

68. S.Freud, *The Future of an Illusion*, in *Complete Works 21. Civilization, Society and Religion,* London 1961, 30.

69. For a discussion of Sigmund Freud see DGE, C III: 'God - an infantile illusion? Sigmund Freud'; also my *Freud und die Zukunft der Religion*, Munich 1987.

70. It is worth noting that so sceptical a philosopher as MacIntyre, at the end of his critical work *After Virtue,* which I have already cited, appeals to St Benedict - doubtless very different - for moral renewal for the present 'dark ages' (comparable to the time after the collapse of the Roman imperial power): 'What matters at this stage is the construction of local forms of community within which civility and the intellectual and moral life can be sustained through the new dark ages which are already upon us. And if the tradition of the virtues was able to survive the horrors of the last dark ages, we are not entirely without grounds for hope. This time however the barbarians are not waiting beyond the frontiers; they have already been governing us for quite some time. And it is our lack of consciousness of this that constitutes part of our predicament. We are waiting not for a Godot, but for another - doubtless very different - St Benedict' (245).

71. For a discussion of Nietzsche's nihilism see DGE, Part D: 'Nihilism - Consequence of Atheism'. H.Lübbe, *Religion nach der Aufklärung*, Graz 1986, has serious grappled with the problems of religion from the standpoint of philosophy. There is much valuable material in the two volumes on religion and philosophy edited by W.Oelmüller, Vol.1, *Wiederkehr von Religion? Perspektiven, Argumente, Fragen,* Paderborn 1984; Vol.2, *Wahrheitsansprüche der Religionen heute*, Paderborn 1986. Cf. also P.Koslowski (ed.), *Die*

religiöse Dimension der Gesellschaft. Religionen und ihre Theorien, Tübingen 1985.

72. On this see also DGE, C II: 'God - A consolation serving vested interests? Karl Marx'.

73. The significance of religion in the context of a global analysis is emphatically stressed by E.Laszlo: 'Narrow-mindedness has with very few exceptions often defeated or damaged the efforts of institutional religion. Rivalries and "holy wars", between Jews and Muslims, Catholics and Protestants, Buddhists and Christians, "believers" and "heathen" in general have excited people, led to senseless sacrifices and engendered heedless violence. But if the great religions made room for their innate ecumenism, they could communicate the spirit of solidarity, toleration and unity in present-day culture' (ibid., 139).

74. For Feuerbach's projection argument see DGE, C I: 'God - a projection of man? Ludwig Feuerbach'.

75. Habermas, *Nachmetaphysiches Denken* (n.66), 23.

76. Here I am following the formulations of the Tübingen ethicist Dietmar Mieth. Cf. his article 'Theological and Ethical Reflections on Bioethics', in *Concilium* 203, 1989, 26-38 (the whole issues is devoted to the theme *Ethics in the Natural Sciences*).

77. Because theological ethics has largely accepted autonomous ethics, I have given an account with particular reference to Catholic ethicists like A.Auer, F.Böckle, J.Gründel, W.Korff, D.Mieth and B.Schüller in OBC, D II.1, and DGE E II 3; F IV 4. A good synthesis is provided by F.Böckle, *Fundamentalmoral*, Munich 1977; basic questions of contemporary ethics are also discussed in the first volume of the ecumenical *Handbuch der christlichen Ethik* (three vols.), edited by A.Hertz, W.Korff, T.Rendtorff and H.Ringeling, Freiburg and Gütersloh 1978-1982. Conversely, however, I have not been able to establish that the same ethicists of predominantly Catholic provenance - whose reflections on what is specifically Christian are often vague and ignore historical criticism - would have taken up constructively the suggestions for a clarification of what is specifically Christian as set out in detail in OBC, D II 2 and DGE, III.2. My view is that historical-critical exegesis calls not only for a dogmatics with a historical-critical foundation but also for a theological ethics which is safeguarded by historical criticism.

78. That is how Hans Jonas put the basic question at the congress on 'Ethics and Politics Today' at the University of Kiel (on the initiative of Prime Minister Björn Engholm and the Pax group on 22 February 1990). The great conceptual effort which so significant a philosopher had to exert simply to give a rational foundation for the first imperative of his ethics of survival, namely 'that there should be a humanity' (*Prinzip Verantwortung*, 91), that no statesman should be allowed 'to play dangerous games with humankind' (ibid.) and to want an 'end of the human race', even though it might be deserved (36), must give

food for thought. For my part, I would prefer to assent to Jonas' previous suggestion rather than to this line of argument. That 'humankind does not have the right to suicide' (80), is 'not easy to justify and perhaps cannot be justified at all without religion' (36); the 'unconditional obligation of humankind to exist' (80) and thus 'the obligation... to procreation' (86) cannot be derived from an alien law, as there is no legal subject for it - 'unless this is a law of the creator God for his creatures, to whom is entrusted this continuation of his work along with the bestowing of existence' (86). I can only agree with Hans Jonas when he says 'that religious faith already has answers here which philosophy has to look for, with uncertain prospects of success' (94). I also agree with him when he says that 'faith can therefore very well provide the foundation for ethics, but it is not there on demand' (94). But I am of the opinion that this belief in God is not at all 'absent', but again publicly present today; that it is not 'discredited', as in the modern period, but in postmodernity has now become reasonably responsible, once again worthy of belief.

79. At the Kiel Congress the Heidelberg ethicist Wolfgang Huber argued against Hans Jonas 'that the word "responsibility" has the two senses of accountability and concern for. It contains within itself the twofold question, before whom and for whom responsibility is to be had. Since in his original draft Hans Jonas does not make the religious foundation of responsibility a theme, in his work only the aspect of responsibility for comes into view. So he thinks of responsibility as a one-sided non-reciprocal relationship: for him the characteristic examples are the responsibility of parents for their children and the representative action of the "statesman" for his subjects. This sometimes gives his discussion of the concept of responsibility an elitist, non-democratic slant. This can best be overcome if one considers the twofold relationality of responsibiity. That leads to a reciprocal and dialogical conception of reality instead of to a concept of "total" responsibility. Moreover, there is a place in this for the reciprocal openness of cultures and religions to one another, without which a future world ethic is unthinkable.' On this see W.Huber's collection of articles, *Konflikt und Konsens. Studien zur Ethik der Verantwortung*, Munich 1990.

80. As sociologists are approaching the problems of religion in a critical and constructive way: to mention just some recent works, P.L.Berger, *The Social Construction of Reality*, New York 1966; id., *The Sacred Canopy. Elements of a Sociological Theory of Religion*, New York 1967; id., *A Rumor of Angels. Modern Society and the Rediscovery of the Supernatural*, New York 1969 and London 1970; F.X.Kaufmann, *Religion und Modernität. Sozialwissenschaftliche Perspektiven*, Tübingen 1989 (I note important agreements with my view particularly in ch.10: 'Ist das Christentum zukunftsfähig?') and, in the framework of his functional theory of social systems, N.Luhmann, *Funktion der Religion*, Frankfurt 1977; id., 'Society, Meaning, Religion - Based on Self-Reference', in *Sociological Analysis* 46, 1985, 5-20 (the whole issue is

devoted to Luhmann's understanding of religion).

81. On this see CWR and CR. At this point I would like to thank all my colleagues in these books, J.van Ess, H.von Stietencron, H.Bechert and above all Julia Ching for the innumerable insights which I have gained in conversation and work with them.

82. For the ethics of the world religions cf. C.H.Ratschow (ed.), *Ethik der Weltreligionen. Ein Handbuch. Primitive Hinduismus, Buddhismus, Islam,* Stuttgart 1980; P.Antes et al., *Ethik in nichtchristlichen Kulturen,* Stuttgart 1984. See also the series *Ethik der Religionen - Lehre und Leben,* edited by M.Klöcker and U.Tworuschka, Munich and Göttingen 1984ff. The volumes which have appeared so far deal with sexuality, work, health, possessions and poverty, and the environment.

83. I have discussed the situation-related validity of norms in OBC, D II, 1, 'Norms of the human'.

84. Confucius, *Analects,* 15.23.

85. Rabbi Hillel, *Shabbat* 31a.

86. Matthew 7.12; Luke 6.31.

87. I.Kant, *Critique of Practical Reason,* A 54.

88. Ibid., *Groundwork of the Metaphysics of Ethics,* BA 66f.

89. H.Jonas, 'Dankesrede anlässlich der Verleihung des Friedenspreises des Deutschen Buchhandels am 11. Oktober 1984', in the collection of his papers, *Wissenschaft als persönliches Erlebnis,* Göttingen 1987, 39.

90. A.Rich, 'Wirtschaft aus christlicher Sicht (Bericht)', in *Luzerner Tagblatt,* 20 January 1990. Cf. id., *Wirtschaftsethik. Grundlagen in theologischer Perspektive,* Gütersloh ³1987.

91. Cf. F.Hengsbach, 'Gegen die Blockade. Soziale Bewegungen haben den Kapitalismus ethisch verwandelt', *Die Zeit,* 21 April 1989.

92. I owe valuable insights into a world ethic to an inter-disciplinary seminar in the winter semester of 1989/90 at the University of Tübingen with the Tübingen Catholic ethicist, Gerfried Hunold, who in the handbook of Christian ethics mentioned above has in particular discussed questions of its material basis (cf. Vol.I, 126-34, 177-95). Cf. similarly G.W.Hunold and W.Korff (eds.), *Die Welt für morgen. Ethische Herausforderungen im Anspruch der Zukunft,* Munich 1986, especially Chapter IX, 'Die interkulturell-religiöse Herausforderung' (H.Waldenfels, K.-W.Merks and H.Bürkle), 357-89.

93. *Religion for Peace: Proceedings of the Kyoto Conference on Religion and Peace,* ed. Homer A. Jack, New Delhi and Bombay 1973, p.ix

94. *'Frieden in Gerechtigkeit für die ganze Schöpfung.' Texte der Europäischen Ökumenischen Versammlung Frieden in Gerechtigkeit, Basel 15.-21. Mai 1989* and of the forum *'Gerechtigkeit, Frieden und Bewahrung der Schöpfung' der Arbeitsgemeinschaft christlicher Kirchen in der Bundesrepublik Deutschland und Berlin (West) e.V., Stuttgart 20.-22. Oktober 1988,* edited by the Kirchenamt der Evangelischen Kirche in Deutschland (EKD), Hanover.

95. Cf. ibid., 24.

96. Cf. ibid., 25-27. Of course postmodern requirements formulated in this European context would have to be modified for other countries and continents. However, the urgency of these requirements is shown particularly by a continent like Latin America, to which we were only able to pay marginal attention, but where experts speak 'of a permanent social and ecological crisis which in certain sectors and regions is taking on the character of downright catastrophe'. Thus, with vast amounts of information, M.Wöhlcke, *Der Fall Lateinamerika. Die Kosten des Fortschritts*, Munich 1989, 116.

97. I have developed the hermeneutical presuppositions of this strategy at length in TA, C II: the following theses were tested at a symposium organized at Temple University in Philadelphia by my colleague Leonard Swidler, in discussion with Wilfred Cantwell Smith, Raymondo Panikkar and John Cobb. Cf. L.Swidler (ed.), *Toward a Universal Theology of Religion*, New York 1987.

98. Cf. the criticism of this theory in OBC, A III 2, 'Anonymous Christianity?'

99. See the criticism in CWR, B I 2, 'Is there the one mystical experience?'

100. Cf. H.-J.Loth, M.Mildenberger and U.Tworuschka, *Christentum im Spiegel der Weltreligionen. Kritische Texte und Kommentare*, Stuttgart 1978.

101. Cf. J.G.Stoessinger, *Why Nations Go to War*, London [4]1985.

102. Cf.W.Korff, *Norm und Sittlichkeit. Untersuchungen zur Logik der normativen Vernunft*, Mainz 1973; id., *Wie kann der Mensch glücken? Perspektiven der Ethik*, Munich 1985.

103. Cf. the summary report of the Paris conference by my Tübingen colleague Karl-Josef Kuschel, 'Weltreligionen und Menschenrechte', *Evangelische Kommentare* 22, 1989, 17-19.

104. I am grateful to the representatives of the various religions, above all to the professors who gave the main papers at the UNESCO colloquium: Masao Abe, Kyoto (Buddhism); Mohammed Arkoun, Paris (Islam); Eugene B.Borowitz, New York (Judaism); Claude Geffré, Paris (Christianity); Liu Shu-hsien, Hong Kong (Confucianism); and Bithika Mukerji, Benares (Hinduism).

105. In what follows I quote the so far unpublished acts of the Paris colloquium.

106. On this see my 'Dialogfestigkeit und Standfestigkeit. Über zwei komplementäre Tugenden', *Evangelische Theologie* 49, 492-504, and the thematic volume *Christianity among the World Religions*, edited by H.Küng and J.Moltmann, *Concilium* 183, 1987.

107. Indeed already among the Greeks (*andreia* in Plato and Aristotle, and also *karteria* in the Stoa) and the Latins (*fortitudo* in Cicero and Macrobius) the word bravery covered a whole semantic field: from a more passive form of acceptance and endurance, resistance and persistance, to more active forms

154

of resolute enterprise and controversy. Certainly the New Testament has no direct acquaintance with concepts like *andreia* and *karteria*, but it has parallels to these concepts: hope (*elpis*), steadfastness (*hypomone*), patience (*makrothymia*), grounded in trusting faith (*pistis*).

Thomas Aquinas then stressed bravery as a special moral virtue and defined it as steadfastness for the good, as proving the self in the difficult tasks, dangers and sufferings of life: 'Firmness of mind (*firmitas animi*) in enduring and repulsing whatever makes steadfastness outstandingly difficult; that is, particularly serious dangers' (*Summa theologiae* II-II q.123 a.2). So steadfastness is another name for bravery, just as civil courage might be today. But whereas civil courage applies more to individual actions in the political and social sphere, steadfastness defines the whole life of a person as a basic spiritual attitude.

108. Thomas Aquinas, who transformed the ancient Roman virtue in a Christian direction, sees *constantia* (like the *perseverantia* which is akin to it) as a component virtue of bravery: 'a firm persistence in the good' (*persistendo firmiter in bono*, q. 137. a.3), against inner weariness and temptation, and against external difficulties and obstacles. This virtue has a central place not only in the 'steadfast prince' Calderon and in the dramas of the French classical playwright Corneille, but also in the 'Be steadfast' of Mozart's *Magic Flute*.

109. Cf. Paul Knitter, *No Other Name? A Critical Survey of Christian Attitudes toward the World Religions*, Maryknoll and London 1985; J.Hick and P.Knitter (eds.), *The Myth of Christian Uniqueness. Toward a Pluralistic Theology of Religions*, New York and London 1987. Professor Knitter had an opportunity to present his arguments in a lecture to the University of Tübingen on 20 November 1989 and discuss them publicly with my Protestant colleagues Eberhard Jüngel and Jürgen Moltmann and myself. For this see the issue of *Evangelische Theologie* 49, 1989, vol.6, on 'Dialog der Religionen?', edited by J.Moltmann.

110. Cf. I Corinthians 12.3.

111. Cf. John 14.6.

112. Cf. P.Tillich, *Christianity and the Encounter of the World Religions*, New York 1963, 36f.: 'This astonishing universalism [of early Christianity], however, was always balanced by a criterion which was never questioned, either by the orthodox or by the heretical groups: the image of Jesus as the Christ, as documented in the New, and prepared for in the Old Testament. Christian universalism was not syncretistic; it did not mix, but rather subjected whatever it received to an ultimate criterion. In the power of this polarity between universality and concreteness it entered the Medieval period, having to compete with no religion equal to it in either of these respects.'

113. Cf J.Cobb. *Beyond Dialogue. Toward a Mutual Transformation of Christianity and Buddhism*, Philadelphia 1982.

114. I am grateful to the Robert Bosch Jubilee Foundation for supporting

155

this research project for five years.

115. Cf. F.Stern (ed.), *The Varieties of History*, Cleveland, Ohio 1956.

116. The *World Christian Encyclopedia. A Comparative Study of Churches and Religions in the Modern World, AD 1900-2000*, Nairobi, Oxford and New York 1982, edited by D.B.Barrett with a wealth of statistical material, offers a survey of Christianity and the religions in 223 countries.

117. For G.W.F.Hegel's view of history cf. - along with *Aesthetics. Lectures on Fine Art* (Oxford 1975) and the *Lectures on the History of Philosophy* (3 vols., London 1892) - above all the *Lectures on the Philosophy of World History* (Cambridge 1975) and the *Lectures on the Philosophy of Religion* (London 1896). For interpretation and literature see IG.

118. Cf. K.Marx and F.Engels, *Manifesto of the Communist Party*, in *Collected Works*, Vol. 6, London 1976, 477-519; K.Marx, *A Contribution to the Critique of Political Economy*, in *Collected Works*, Vol. 29, London 1987, especially the Preface, 261-5; F.Engels, *Anti-Dühring, Collected Works*, Vol 25, London 1987, 5-315.

119. Cf. O.Spengler, *The Decline of the West* (two vols.), London 1926-28. Following A.M.Koktanek's biography, *O.Spengler in seiner Zeit*, Munich 1968, D.Felken brings out the significance of Spengler for politics and the history of ideas: O.Spengler, *Konservativer Denker zwischen Kaiserreich und Diktatur*, Munich 1989.

120. Spengler, *Decline* (n.119), Vol.2, 304.

121. Ibid., 323.

122. Cf. A.Toynbee, *A Study of History*, I-XII, Oxford 1934-61.

123. Cf. id., *An Historian's Approach to Religion*, London 1956.

124. Cf. A.Toynbee and D.Ikeda, *Choose Life. A Dialogue*, London 1976.

125. Toynbee, *A Study of History*, V, 1939, 126.

126. There is a balanced account of the discussion at the time in P.Kaupp, *Toynbee und die Juden. Eine kritische Untersuchung der Darstellung des Judentums im Gesamtwerk A.J.Toynbees*, Meisenheim, Glan 1967.

127. N.Smart, 'The Study and Classification of Religion', *The New Encyclopedia Britannica* 26, Chicago 1987, 548-62: 552. The American sociologist of religion J.Milton Yinger, *The Scientific Study of Religion*, London and New York 1970, shows this multidisciplinary approach.

128. Cf.M.Eliade, *History of Religious Ideas* (three vols.), Chicago 1979-86.

129. Cf. P.Tillich, 'The Significance of the History of Religions for the Systematic Theologian', in *The Future of Religions. In Memory of Paul Tillich*, ed. J.C.Brauer, New York 1966.

130. Cf. id., *Christianity and the Encounter* (n.112), New York 1963, 53-75.

131. T.S.Kuhn, *The Structure of Scientific Religions*, Chicago 1962; id, *Essential Tension: Selected Studies in Scientific Tradition*, Chicago 1978.

132. For the discussion between Kuhn and his Popperian critics see above

all the volume edited by I.Lakatos and A.Musgrave, *Criticism and the Growth of Knowledge*, London 1970; Kuhn's responses are particularly important here.

133. Cf. G.Gutting, *Paradigms and Revolutions. Appraisals and Applications of Thomas S.Kuhn's Philosophy of Science*, Notre Dame and London 1980; the contributions by D.Hollinger and I.Barbour are particularly important for the problems with which we are concerned, of the possibility of applying Kuhn's analyses to historiography and theology.

134. Cf. TM, especially B, 'Perspectives Forward'.

135. Cf. H.Küng and D.Tracy, *Paradigm Change in Theology*, Edinburgh 1989.

136. Cf. CWR, most clearly in C, 'Buddhism and Christianity'.

137. So defined in the retrospect on the discussion of T.S.Kuhn in his 'Postscript 1969'.

138. Cf. TM B II: 'Paradigm Shift in Theology and Science'.

139. For the basis of this tripartite typology ('ideal types' in the 'chaos of facts', M.Weber), which supplements the double typology of Nathan Söderblom, Friedrich Heiler and Rudolf Otto, etc. (cf. DGE G I2), with the wisdom type, cf. CWR B I2, 'Mystical and Prophetic Religion', and CR, introduction: 'China - A Third Religious Current System'.

140. Cf. *Church*, I.4: OBC, B III; DGE, G I.2; EL, B IV; CWR, A.

141. Cf. DGE, G I.1-2; CWR, B-C.

142. Cf. DGE, G I.1-2; CWR. Recently the American sociologist P.Berger, in an illuminating symposium *The Other Side of God. A Polarity in World Religions,* New York 1981, has suggested the expression 'religions of confrontation' for the prophetic religions and 'religions of interiority' for the mystical religions. These are categories to be used in a differentiated way, and I gladly adopt them here for a more accurate definition. However, even in Berger's composite volume the third, wisdom type of Chinese religions, 'religions of harmony', is missing.

143. Cf. M.Weber, *Gesammelte Aufsätze zur Religionssoziologie*, Vols I-III, Tübingen 1920.

144. Cf. W.E.Hocking, *Living Religions and a World Faith*, New York 1940.

145. For Vivekananda the eternal principle (*sanatana dharma*) of the Hindu tradition, as distinct from the social principle (*svadharmna*) as expressed in the caste tradition, stands over all creeds and religions: 'Do not care for doctrines, do not care for dogmas, or sects, or churches, or temples: they count for little compared with the essence of existence in each man which is spirituality' (*Speeches and Writings of Swami Vivekananda*, Madras nd, 31); quoted in J.M.Kitagawa, *The 1893 World's Parliament of Religions and its Legacy*, Chicago 1983.

146. S.Radhakrishnan, *Eastern Religions and Western Thought*, London

1939; cf. DGE G I 2, 'All equally true?'.

147. See the report on the working party of the sub-unit 'Dialogue with People of Other Religions' of the World Council of Churches for the Potsdam conference of 13-20 July 1986, Diana L.Eck, 'Interreligöser Dialog - was ist damit gemeint? Ein Überblick über die verschiedenen Formen des interreligiösen Dialogs', *Una Sancta* 43, 1988, 189-200.

148. With the focus of 'Christianity and Islam', religion as a factor of education for peace was the theme of the third Nuremberg Forum. Cf. the numerous contributions in J.Lähnemann (ed.), *Weltreligionen und Friedenserziehung. Wege zur Toleranz*, Hamburg 1989. The volume edited by U.Schmidt from an educational perspective, with particular reference to the Third World, *Kulturelle Identität und Universalität. Interkulturelles Lernen als Bildungsprinzip*, Frankfurt 1986, takes a similar line (see especially the articles by P.V.Dias, A.Imfeld and G.Flaig).